LIVING in the PAST

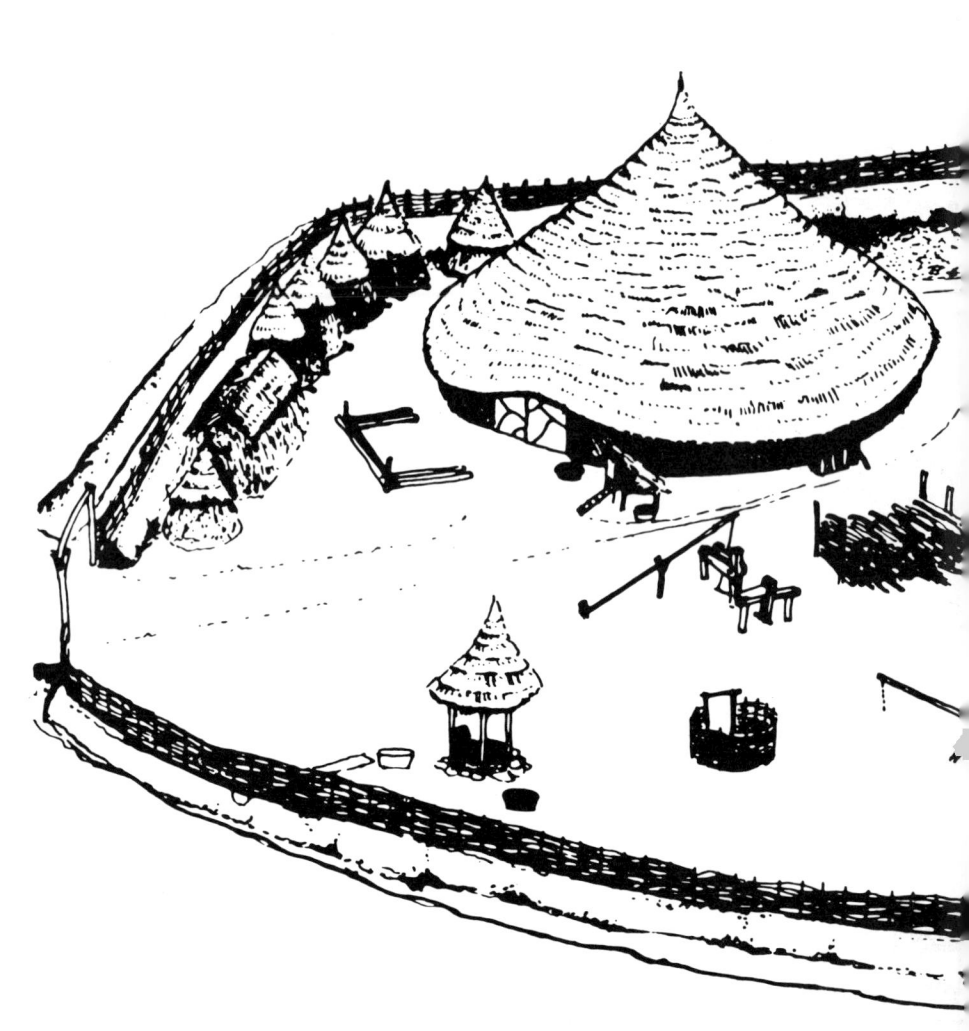

LIVING
in the PAST

John Percival

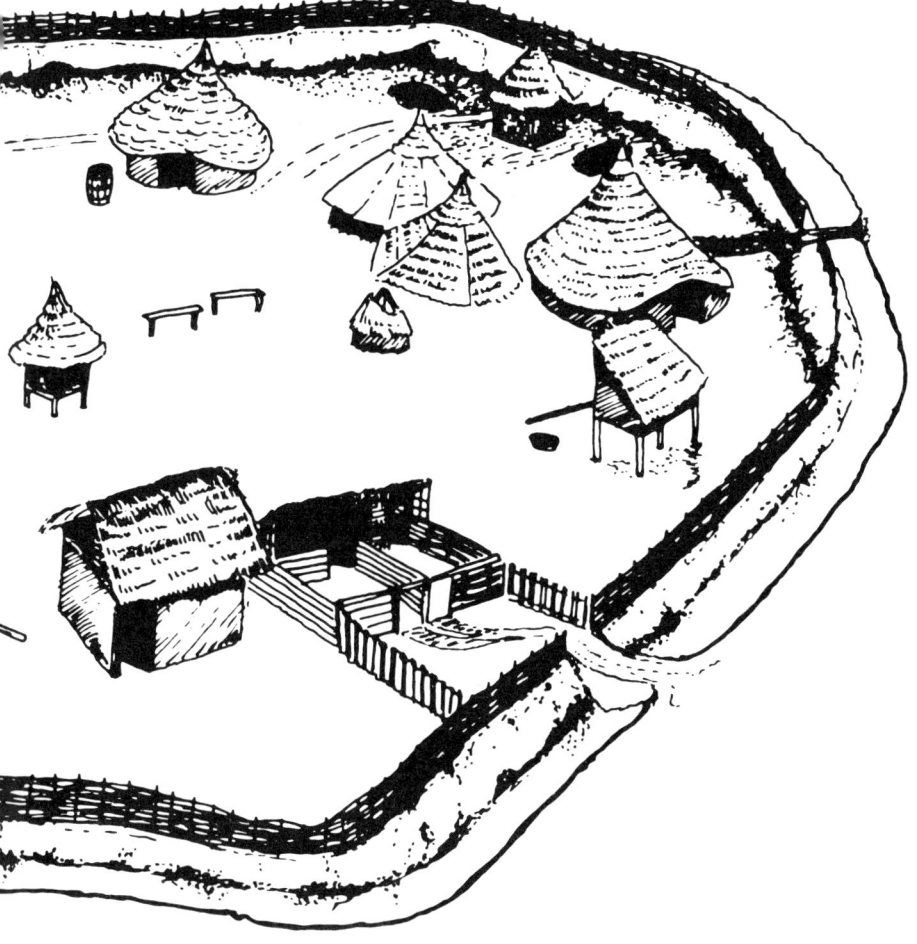

BRITISH BROADCASTING CORPORATION

Illustrations by Brian Ackroyd;
photographs on pages 15, 39,
77, 82, 106, 156, 163 and 172
by Digby Elliott; all remaining
pictures are BBC copyright
photographs by David Edwards
and John Percival.

Published by the
British Broadcasting Corporation,
35 Marylebone High Street,
London W1M 4AA

ISBN 0 563 17517 6

First published 1980
© John Percival 1980

Printed in England by
Ebenezer Baylis & Son Ltd,
The Trinity Press,
Worcester, and London.

Contents

The volunteers Back row, left to right: **the two Peter Ainsworths,
father and son, Martin Elphick, Peter Little** (holding a greylag
goose), **John Rossetti, Brian Ackroyd and John Rockliff** (with
Annabelle). Front row, left to right: **Lindsay Ainsworth with Robin,
Helen Elphick, Sarah Rockliff, Jill Grainger, Kate Rossetti, Nicholas
Ainsworth, Sharon Preston**, and the dogs Sirius and Emer.

Chapter One

I first had the idea for the Iron Age project sitting on a wet hillside on Exmoor, wet, hungry and wretchedly uncomfortable. Together with a small group of other enthusiasts for the simple life I was taking part in an experiment for a television programme, to see if it was possible for people to live off the land with nothing to help them but a knife and a piece of string. It rained all day and most of the night for two solid weeks. We built our rather leaky shelter, caught a few rabbits and ate a lot of mushrooms and blackberries, but never enough; the shelter was inadequate and it was a mercy that the experiment lasted only two weeks because we were all slowly starving to death and dying of exposure, both at the same time. What a pity, I thought as I sat there, cold and hungry, exposing myself to the elements, that we do not now understand what primitive men and women understood. They would have made themselves warm and comfortable, would have found enough food and would probably have found time to enjoy themselves as well. Would it be possible, I wondered, for modern people to re-adapt to those conditions, to rediscover the ancient skills and learn to prosper within the limits of a simple technology?

The idea remained vague and half-formed until I happened to be in Denmark a year or two later and heard about the open-air museum at Lejre, run by an archaeologist named Hans Olle Hansen. Hansen has built a reconstruction of a Danish Iron Age village, complete with livestock, tools, a small area of agricultural land. Every year he invites a few families to stay in one of the houses for a couple of weeks, to show themselves off to the tourists and play about with Iron Age tools and pottery. This was the idea that I had been looking for, without the tourists of course, and for a long enough period of time to allow people to exercise their ingenuity by trial and error.

The period of prehistory in which the Danish experiment was set also appealed to me because I knew that it was well documented. The Iron Age is a label of convenience adopted by nineteenth-century archaeologists to describe a certain stage of metallurgical development. In Europe it is usually taken to cover that period of time from the development of the Hallstat culture in Austria, and the introduction of iron around 800 B.C., up to the establishment of Roman dominion over most of the Continent and the offshore British Isles. The later phases of the Iron Age, the culture known as La Tène after a famous site in Switzerland, produced some extraordinary works of art. On the Continent, particularly in France, metal work of exquisite quality has been found, bronze bowls and ewers, with a flowing stylised ornamentation of mythical beasts and plants. In Britain there developed a more abstract insular style, weapons, shields and mirrors with curling scroll work and delicate enamelling.

These fine pieces were the treasures of a warrior aristocracy. The Iron Age Europeans were Celts, a scattering of many tribes and peoples who shared a common language and occupied a territory stretching from Central Turkey in the East to Ireland in the West, an area almost as extensive as the Roman Empire at its height. But the Celts were not a united people. Although warlike their warfare was an affair of individual heroism, acts of daring machismo, single combat between warrior heroes. They defeated the Romans more than once but they never had the organisation to stay on top for very long. Instead they expended their energies in tribal squabbles and their haphazard style of fighting was eventually no match for the disciplined Roman legions. In the last phase of their supremacy in Europe the Celts built fortified towns of considerable size, with rows of houses laid out in streets and massive fortifications of timber and stone. The ramparts which surrounded them still stand on many hilltops, the vertical walls and deep ditches now just grassy undulations in the ground. These so-called hill forts varied greatly in use. They were castles in time of war, but they also appear to have been centres for political administration and for trade. There is evidence, for instance, that the organised export of grain from Britain to France was in operation by the first century B.C. The Gauls in France exported wine to Britain, British hunting dogs were famous in Europe and many of the Celtic tribes eventually had their own coinage as a medium of exchange.

All this, of course, suggests a degree of sophistication and a scale of building which would be far too ambitious to reproduce. But the glamour of the art, the warrior confrontations, even the great Celtic citadels, with their suggestion of organised labour on a vast scale, all this has to be envisaged against a background of simple agriculture. All around the towns then, as now, were small farmsteads, little villages perhaps, each occupied by a single extended family or a small group of families. The people were farmers, raising livestock, tilling the land, and it was on the surplus that they could produce that the whole of the rest of the pyramid was built. It was one of these communities then, a hamlet no bigger than Hansen's little collection of huts at Lejre, that I wanted to try to recreate.

Back in England, I discovered that much of the background research had already been done. Peter Reynolds, a maverick classical scholar with a bent for archaeology, runs a project called the Butser Ancient Farm at the Queen Elizabeth Country Park in Hampshire. The aims of the farm are scholarly and scientific. Reynolds and his partner, Jack Langley, are concerned to discover how Iron Age farmers in Britain managed their agriculture, built their houses, made their tools and equipment. It is no part of their responsibility to try and *live* within the limits of an Iron Age environment, nor would it be possible for them to conduct accurate scientific experiments while doing so. But in the course of their experiments they have produced answers to many of the problems which would have been baffling to a comparative layman like myself. Working from reports of many different excavations and using a great variety of material, historical and ethnographic as well as archaeological, Peter Reynolds is slowly building up a picture of what everyday life was like in Iron Age Britain. His work is necessarily incomplete, many of his findings are tentative, because the information on which they are based is sadly deficient, but with very slender resources and formidable determination, he and Jack Langley have come up with some remarkable results.

The academic world is full of jealousies and honest differences of opinion. Not everyone accepts everything that the Butser project has demonstrated. But when I came to draw up my plans for the Iron Age village I relied heavily on Reynolds and Langley for advice. It was they and the team of expert advisers on the Committee for Ancient Agriculture, who suggested the most suitable livestock, who provided blueprints for the houses, who advised on all manner of tools and techniques. It was obvious that between them they knew far more about Iron Age Britain than I could ever hope to find out by reading books or visiting museums. But at the same time I believed, and still believe, that to get a group of volunteers actually living in the houses, depending on the crops and the livestock for their subsistence, relying on the tools for their livelihood would bring a new dimension to our understanding of prehistory. It is not enough to know how a job may have been done; it is not enough even to do the job oneself and repeat the demonstration, with all the monitoring devices, the weighing and measuring and timing that scientific experimental archaeology demands. It is necessary to do the job day after day, to depend upon its being done satisfactorily to fulfil your everyday needs. It is necessary to live an experience in order fully to comprehend it.

What I proposed therefore was to gather together a group of ten or twelve volunteers, with children if possible, and invite them to spend a year building and then living in a reconstruction of a prehistoric British farm, one of the many thousands of homesteads scattered across the south of England about a hundred and fifty years before the birth of Christ. The volunteers would be given as much help as possible before the project started; they would be given an introduction to the crafts and skills that the Iron Age Celts are known to have practised and they would be supplied with livestock, seed, tools and equipment appropriate to the period. But once the village was a going concern, the outside help would be withdrawn and they would be left to themselves, apart of course from the visits of the television unit.

First reactions to the idea from senior colleagues at the BBC were understandably sceptical. How could volunteers be found? Would they stick it out? Would there be any danger of their suffering physically or psychologically from the experience? How much would it all cost? It is a tribute to their far-sightedness that they did not cry off altogether. After a good deal of hard research and as many safeguards as I could provide, the project was given a cautious go-ahead.

At first the production team was minimal, my assistant, Linda Cleeve, and myself. I toured the western counties at weekends and on days off, searching for a suitable site. Linda tracked down hundreds of suppliers of everything from timber to pigs' bristle, from potters' clay to rawhide, in search of materials. Between us we also located craftsmen, men who understood the ancient skills of basket making, weaving, leather and woodwork, the thatcher and the potter, the beekeeper and the blacksmith.

We also sought the advice of many different archaeologists, visited dozens of museums, collected piles of obscure papers on wool fibres and lost wax bronze casting. We wrote dozens of letters to possible suppliers of primitive sheep and cattle.

Most of the advice on livestock stemmed originally from Professor Peter Jewell, a zoologist who has also given a great deal of attention to the bone remains from prehistoric sites. He advised us to acquire sheep known as Soays, from the island where they were first identified. They are small, brown or meal coloured, they can jump like jack rabbits, and their bones are virtually indistinguishable from sheep bones found in Iron Age rubbish pits. Peter Jewell also suggested Dexter cattle, a miniature breed from Ireland. Pedigree specimens have very short legs, but mongrel animals, the kind we were after, have longer legs and closely resemble *Bos Longifrons*, the Iron Age cow. The hunt was also on for the right kind of goats, pigs, chickens and geese.

I was still looking for a location. Ideally, it had to be close enough to my base in Bristol to make the administrative arrangements feasible and yet remote enough to keep away unwanted visitors. There was also the question of suitability from the practical point of view: we needed native woodland that could be exploited for fuel and building materials, some kind of water supply and a secluded area for arable farming. The site I eventually discovered had all of these qualities and many others besides, not the least of which was that the landlord looked kindly on the whole idea from the beginning and so too did his friendly and capable land agent, and several other extremely helpful estate employees.

The chalk downland stretches in a broad undulating series of domes and ridges right the way across Southern Britain. Along its highest escarpments run the prehistoric highways, the Ridgeway, the Icknield Way, which are even more ancient than the Iron Age. The chalk is good farmland, with large spreads of wheat and barley on the lower stretches and pasture for cattle and sheep on the high downs. Littered all over the slopes and hilltops are the remains of prehistoric settlements and in those places where the land has remained unploughed for thousands of years, the downs have proved rich in archaeological material. The land in these areas has changed very little since ancient times. There is perhaps a little more timber on the hilltops, a little less in the valleys, and as the water table has dropped many of the springs have dried up. Otherwise the land looks much as it must have done when the Celtic farmers first set their hands to plough the little square fields. It was on one of these great chalk ridges, with an ancient highway passing within half a mile and an Iron Age hill fort almost within sight, that the project was to take place. The location was ideal, a field of about fifteen acres surrounded on all sides by woodland, with a clearing in the woods close by, which made a secluded site for the village.

Suitable or not, there could very easily have been no project at all on that site, or any other, if the Planning Authorities had not been amenable. During my search I had discovered another site in another county which had also seemed in many ways ideal for the project. Full of enthusiasm I went to see the Chief Planning Officer for the area concerned. It must be understood that under existing legislation nobody in Britain is permitted to live in officially substandard accommodation, let alone build it. This particular Planning Officer was not amused by the idea, and referred me to the Building Regulations Officer, who considered the plans with grave deliberation.

'Well, providing that Planning Permission is forthcoming . . .' his tone implied that it would not be . . . 'and provided you can satisfy the Public Health Authorities and the Fire Safety Officer, I see no reason why people should not build and inhabit an Iron Age house, provided –' and here he gave me a look of stern warning – 'that your Iron Age house has cavity walls, a damp proof course, an internal lavatory and bathroom with hot and cold running water and of course a properly ventilated larder.'

Fortunately the Planning Officer for the new location took a more flexible view. 'I suppose we could describe them as agricultural buildings,' he said thoughtfully. 'Anyway, we'll have a quiet word with everybody involved and see whether anyone is likely to object. Provided that nobody does . . .' he would have winked if it had been dignified to do so . . . 'then it will probably take us six months to find out what you're doing and another six months to stop you doing it.' So the main obstacles to the project were overcome, but the most important element of all had still to be found, the people who were going to take part.

In June 1976, as soon as we had a definite go-ahead, we placed an advertisement in the columns of *The Times*. As I had hoped, other newspapers picked it up and almost the whole of Fleet Street ran a few column inches on the project. The response was overwhelming. Letters flooded in from all over the country, eventually from all over the world. In all, we received nearly two thousand applications. There were very few from elderly or middle-aged people. The great bulk were from young people – some very young – and the majority also ignored the terms of the original advertisement and offered themselves alone, without a partner.

I had an alarming and slightly prurient vision of a dozen young people who had hardly met each other before, settling down to live in the closest proximity for twelve months. It would take them all their time to sort out their sex lives, I thought, let alone build an Iron Age village. I wanted equal numbers of men and women, but I wanted them in couples, couples who were used to each other, who would support one another when the going got rough, but I did not demand high levels of manual skill or a profound knowledge of prehistory.

After a series of interviews, a short list of twenty candidates, some of them with young children, was selected, and were packed off to spend a week living rough in a field close to the Butser Farm in Hampshire. Here, Peter Reynolds and Jack Langley introduced them to Iron Age tools and techniques and they spent their days labouring and their evenings trying to work out how to live without most modern conveniences, cooking utensils, toilet paper, cosmetics and so on. They also became closely acquainted with one another, since there were only two large tents for twenty-six people. At the end of the week they were invited to fill in what was, in effect, a ballot paper. Each couple was invited to name five other couples, in order of preference, with whom they felt they could most easily spend a year in an Iron Age reconstruction.

The group that emerged from this ballot was therefore to some extent self selecting, a factor which may have helped them overcome their difficulties later on.

When the television programmes eventually appeared the volunteers were criticised for being middle class. If this was true it was only in the sense that they were all people who were capable of responding to a newspaper story and filling in an application form. It was true that most of them had been through some kind of higher education at university or technical college and many of them wanted to pursue a professional career in due course, but by birth they were as mixed a cross-section of people as one could look to find, from the poorest to the relatively prosperous. What probably irritated the reviewers was that almost by definition the volunteers were not the kind of people who were likely to miss the fleshpots of the consumer society too much. They were being paid a flat rate of a thousand pounds a head for appearing in the television programmes and nothing at all for actually taking part in the project. The greedy, the stupid and the faint-hearted were not even likely to apply.

The age range in the group was very narrow. Excluding the Ainsworth children, Kate Rossetti, at twenty-two, was the youngest and Peter Ainsworth, who was thirty, was the eldest. I would have liked to have had a couple of village elders in the community, but there had been a severe dearth of elderly applicants for a year without ventilated larders and damp courses. What we did have was a wide range of talents. Pete Ainsworth had spent some years as a working farmer and John Rockliff had been a jobbing builder, Martin Elphick had just qualified as a doctor and the other men had all been used to working with their hands as well as their brains. Three of the women had been teachers, which meant that they had some basic experience of handicrafts. Helen Elphick was a trained nurse, Lindsay Ainsworth a hairdresser and Sharon Preston had done so many different jobs in her short life that she would obviously adapt to anything.

The volunteers were not the only people essential to the project. I had also recruited Brian Hawkins, a genial kindly man in his early forties, vastly experienced in television, as Assistant Producer. He, together with Linda Cleeve and myself, made up the production team. We also contracted a film crew, who all became closely involved with the project – David Saunders, the cameraman, Tom Brown, the sound recordist and Digby Elliott, assistant, though as time went by his place was taken by Trevor Adamson. The film editor, Tom Poore, was also an essential member of the team and he, together with his assistant Dave Mitchell, were among the most frequent visitors to the project. But at one time or another, hundreds of people were involved with provisions and preparations. There were splendid old craftsmen – like Ted Hart, blacksmith – who preserve a folk memory of techniques of craftsmanship which are centuries old. Skills like his were essential to the training of the volunteers.

For the five months following their initial selection, throughout the autumn and winter of 1976/77, the volunteers were given the opportunity to spend their spare time learning a number of basic crafts – blacksmithing, weaving, pottery – essential to life in Iron Age conditions. The choice was left to the individuals. Interestingly but predictably, only men chose to learn the craft of the blacksmith. Only women, on the other hand, chose to do weaving. But there was some breakdown in sexual roles. Three of the girls, Lindsay, Kate and Jill, went down to Somerset to learn basket weaving, which was always a male preserve in the West of England. Sharon and Helen chose to work with leather, and this is also traditionally a man's job, especially the heavy and smelly labour of fleshing hides and tanning.

The volunteers all spent a few days on a farm, getting accustomed to working with animals and with traditional agricultural tools. They were also given an introduction to the archaeology of the period and one or two weekend courses in plant recognition, hunting and tracking and impromptu building techniques. At the end of this brief course of training they were expected to undertake the year-long experiment with the minimum of outside help. It was a difficult assignment, but

Reconstructions of Iron Age tools, with the exception of the axe,
top right, **which is of a modern design.**

had it not been so, had they not gone in cold, as it were, with the
minimum of training, they would no longer have been modern young
people at all, and modern people, with all the confusions and lack of
preparedness that life in today's world entails, were the necessary
guinea-pigs if the whole experiment was to have any meaning at all.

What we set out to do – and this has been much misunderstood –
was to see if a group of quite ordinary young people, most of them
born and brought up in towns, could learn to live successfully within
the limits of an Iron Age technology. It was clearly impossible to
recapture the beliefs and superstitions, the skills and experience, the
basic social attitudes of prehistoric people and this was never our
intention. But what we could do was to recreate the living conditions,
the houses, the clothes, the food and the hard slogging labour which
Iron Age people must have endured, and see if it was possible for
modern people to adapt to those conditions. The pressures on them
would be enormous. They would be cut off from their families, their
friends and from all the comforts and conveniences of modern life.
They would have no music, no entertainment other than that which
they could provide for themselves. They would not even be allowed to

wander freely over the countryside and in this respect as in many others their lot would be far harder than that faced by the original Iron Age farmers two thousand years ago. They had sentenced themselves to a twelve-month prison term in conditions which would outrage any penal reformer the length and breadth of the civilised world and before they could even begin their sentence they had to build their own prison camp.

Chapter Two

It was a cold, blowy February afternoon when the volunteers arrived on the site that was to be their home for the next thirteen months. The leafless branches of the trees round the clearing in the forest tossed and swayed against a grey sky. The dark woods round about and the windswept downs beyond seemed wild and lonely. It did not look at all the kind of place where people would live and work, let alone enjoy life. But with slightly desperate cheerfulness the volunteers set about unpacking the brightly coloured tents and starting a rather smoky fire.

They set up their camp in the woods about two hundred yards from the clearing that had been set aside for the village. The small marquee, cluttered with cardboard boxes, kerosene lamps and butane cooking stoves, stood beside the ride which ran down one side of the fifteen-acre field. The bivouac tents were scattered among the trees round about with the camp fire more or less in the middle. In the February rain the ground between the tents quickly turned into a shallow swamp. The floor of the marquee was soon thick with mud and the volunteers' boots, clothes, even their hair and hands were coated with it. There was nowhere to dry clothes out, nothing to wash in apart from a plastic bowl, no lavatory apart from a shallow hole in the ground and of course none of those aids to cleanliness we normally consider essential like toothbrushes and toilet paper. Every two days or so they were provided with food, a kind of supermarket version of an Iron Age diet: bread, cheese, meat, dried peas and beans, more bread. The whole atmosphere was that of an exceptionally nasty camping holiday when the person in charge has forgotten to bring half the gear.

These were the conditions in which they had to live until the buildings were complete, conditions which I hoped would make the hardships of a prehistoric environment seem relatively luxurious.

The first job was fencing the fifteen-acre field. They had to make sure that at least the area that the animals would graze was securely fenced off from both the forest and the arable land. So, following Peter Reynolds' instructions about Iron Age fences, the volunteers began to drive in hazel posts, about a metre apart, around the perimeter of the field. Hazel wands were then woven in and out between the fence posts making a dense six-foot barrier of wattle, strong enough to keep in a moderately happy cow and high enough to discourage the leaping instincts of Soay sheep wanting to get out and wild deer wanting to get in.

First the posts had to be cut one by one in the woods, sharpened with an axe or billhook, and then driven into the hard ground with a big wooden mallet. The post drivers worked in teams of three – one making holes with a crowbar, the other two following behind and hammering in the posts. One person would hold the stake, rather bravely it sometimes seemed to me, and the other would teeter on top of a barrel, bashing away with the big wooden beetle.

Once the posts were in, the hazel wands had to be woven between them, carefully selecting the right piece for the right place, working along the fence so that the butt ends of each rod tucked neatly in behind a post and each successive length overlapped the one that had gone before. Once a hazel rod was in place it had to be tamped firmly down to make sure there were no tempting gaps left for the probing hooves or horns. It was hard, rather dreary work but there were more rewarding tasks ahead.

In the clearing the ground plan of the village was beginning to take shape. Jack Langley came over and marked out the perimeter of the stockade using an ingenious system of sticks and string, basing the outline as exactly as possible on the plans of a genuine Iron Age village. The first priority was to ensure that the layout and the buildings were as authentic as possible. The second priority was speed, so reluctantly I decided that we would have to use some modern equipment to get the job done in time to keep to our thirteen-month schedule. So we brought in a mechanical excavator to dig the surrounding ditch, with a V cut section about three feet deep. The earth from the ditch was then thrown up all the way round to make a bank on the inside of the perimeter, again about three feet in height.

As the mechanical digger worked its way slowly round, two of the volunteers armed with shovels worked close behind it, throwing up any of the earth that fell back towards the ditch and tamping down the bank to make it solid. In less than two days the job was finished. It would have taken the group, especially if they had been equipped only with Iron Age tools, anything up to a month to do that one job. But the end result was the same. There was a satisfactory bank and ditch enclosing an area a little over an acre, very similar to dozens of Iron

Age sites up and down the country, though rather smaller than most.

A gap was left in the bank and ditch about fifteen feet wide where the entrance would be. Opposite the entrance, the marking pegs for the big round house were laid out. The round house was to be the hub of the whole farm, a big circular dwelling, fifty feet across and twenty-five feet from floor to apex. Such big houses were quite common in Iron Age Britain, although their precise function in ancient times remains in doubt. On some sites the houses were very much smaller. But if the group was to be split up into small units scattered around the compound, it seemed unlikely that they would be able to work closely together. So we decided to follow Peter Reynolds' lead at Butser and to house the whole group under one roof, building wicker-work partitions around the edge of the building to allow a measure of privacy. Peter had given me precise measurements for the timbers we would need and the oak posts were already on the site. Peter and Jack then paced out the ground for us, placing pegs at intervals to mark where the main post holes should be dug and where the outer wall should be built.

However, long before they started work on the big round house the volunteers had already begun to put up some of the smaller buildings. In addition to the rings of post holes marking the sites of circular houses, Iron Age excavations frequently reveal groups of four or six holes arranged in squares and rectangles. Each group of posts could have been the main structural supports for a small hut, or possibly some kind of elevated platform which could have been used for almost anything from a base for a granary to a stage for exposing the dead. So the first two buildings began with one neat square and one neat rectangle of post holes and ended up as a goat house and a chicken house.

There is no way of being certain whether this interpretation is right or wrong. It is quite possible that the Ancient Britons kept their chickens in baskets in the treetops and snuggled up every night with their goats. The only test that could be applied to any theory derived from archaeological evidence was whether it worked. The chicken house, which grew into a rather handsome structure on stilts, proved extremely efficient. The goat house was a failure for goats simply because it was too small for eight horned and aggressive nannies, but it later turned into a first-rate milking parlour for the cows, with a neat little hay loft over. Such is the necessary flexibility of a working farm.

The framework for the two other buildings went up at about the

Peter Little at work on the roof of the goat house, in March. This building was later converted into the cow byre.

same time, a log pigsty and a small round house, based on Iron Age house foundations from the so-called 'lake village' near Glastonbury in Somerset. The round house proved much easier to build than the square and rectangular structures which had to be reinforced with diagonal struts with all the joints mortised in, because although the group were using some basic modern tools – saws, axes and a few chisels – they had to manage without nails, which would have been an expensive luxury in the Iron Age. A small round house on the other hand can be put up with a single ring of fairly light posts hammered into the ground. The rafters are then tied with cord to the tops of the posts and drawn upwards to form a conical roof which is lashed together at the top, rather like a Red Indian tepee. In fact the volunteers chose to mortise some of the rafters to the tops of the posts, just to be on the safe side, but the little hut went up with surprising speed.

Once the rafters were in place they tied lengths of hazel to them, bending the rods to form a series of horizontal rings around the roof, one on top of the other with about ten inches between them. These were the thatching battens. The thatch was combed wheat reed, imported on to the site at vast expense, but the rest of the materials were almost all drawn from the surrounding woodland. The only modern material used for any of the buildings, either at this stage or later, was string. String and rawhide cord of various kinds has turned up on Iron Age and even Bronze Age sites, but the evidence suggests that it would have been in rather short supply. For thatching it is quite possible to use strips of hazel or willow bark and bark strips were used for thatching within living memory, but the group was up against a deadline. The original timetable called for all the buildings to be finished by the first of April, by which time they were supposed to be ready to get rid of all their modern tools and equipment and, as they put it 'go Iron Age'. So they used string, good old-fashioned organic binder twine, but string for all that.

Thatching is an interminable, finger-cutting, hand-freezing business, especially in February and especially for beginners. The technique they used to start with involved breaking the big bundles of thatching straw into smaller ones called yelms, about five inches thick, tying each bundle with a length of string about eighteen inches long and then securing each yelm in turn to the batten, taking a turn around the previous bundle and knotting both tightly together. The thatchers worked round in a circle, beginning at the base of the roof and working upwards, batten by batten, so that each row of bundles overlapped the one beneath. Later on, as they grew more skilled they learned more refined techniques, but thatching was always one of the jobs they disliked most. During the vile February weather it meant standing insecurely on a makeshift ladder, pulling tight, tying, knotting, pulling tight again for hours on end in the cold and wet.

At the end of each day's work they sat around a sputtering fire, trying to unfreeze fingers like uncooked sausages. With anorak hoods pulled up against the never-ending rain and the men's beards matted with the wet they looked like a congregation of half-drowned gnomes. There was no warm refuge at the end of the day, only a wet tent and a soggy sleeping bag. Their jeans and sweaters were caked with half-dried mud and their moods were sometimes as black as the squelching mire in which they lived and worked. But somehow they kept working.

By the end of the first two weeks they had put up the frameworks of four buildings. The first three, despite the differences in shape, all had sturdy timber frames and walls built of wattle, but the fourth building, the pigsty, was different. Because pigs have snouts like bulldozers and will push their way out of almost anything, the volunteers decided to fill in the space between the vertical posts with heavy, split ash logs. For the pigs' sleeping compartment they mortised these into the heavy posts. For the outside run they simply drove in pairs of posts close together and dropped the logs into the gaps.

A few days later the first of the animals arrived. They were two ancient Soay sheep, kindly given to us by the Wool Research Institute near Edinburgh. They were both ewes, nearly at the end of their breeding lives, their ragged brown fleeces half hanging off them, tired and miserable after their long journey. We herded them into a small fold of six-foot hurdles and I wondered whether they would even survive the night. They showed no sign of wanting to eat and huddled wretchedly together in a corner of their pen. Rather to my surprise they were still alive the following day and John Rockliff had even coaxed them into eating a few crushed oats, but they still looked as though they could hardly put one foot in front of another. The following day they were gone. A violent storm during the night had blown down a section of the hurdle fence. Everyone went off on a sheep search, combing the woods and trying to follow their tracks, but the soft ground was full of deer slots, which look remarkably like the prints of sheep, especially in muddy ground, and the two old invalids had disappeared. It was a minor disaster. Not only would the project be short of two Soays but the little beasts would certainly get out on to the downs along with all the superior white sheep belonging to the local farmers. Questions would be asked and we would all look rather silly. Real farmers, even Iron Age farmers, do not just lose their sheep.

I had decided in advance that we would break camp at the end of the first two weeks to give the group a few days' rest. Several people still had to complete arrangements for renting their houses and everyone wanted to bid a year's farewell to family and friends. Privately, I also expected that this was the point at which some of them would choose to withdraw from the project. The first couple of weeks had been tough and in many ways unrewarding. It was all too obvious that there was a long hard slog in front of them before they could even begin to enjoy life in anything resembling Iron Age conditions, so I half expected that when we all came back together again at the beginning of March the group would be smaller and gloomier than before.

Chapter Three

Much to my surprise, everyone came back for more after their week's break. As the little bus carrying the group drove up on to the long sweep of downland leading to the site they spotted two small brown animals grazing on the verge by the side of the road. They were the two missing Soays out, it almost seemed, to welcome them back. However, the welcome was not wholehearted and the two old ewes took flight as soon as the bus came up to them, running like hares, darting and leaping, jinking from side to side to avoid pursuit and generally looking most unlike the pathetic geriatrics that had broken out of the pen. Finally, the driver overtook the panicky little beasts, slewed the bus across the road to block their escape and everybody baled out to catch them and carry them home. After a great deal of rushing about Pete Little collared one that ran into a fence and got its horns caught, and Martin tackled the other as it charged towards him. They took the little sheep into the bus and carried them back in triumph to the camp.

Everything was better than it had been. The weather was much drier, though a damp fog continued to cling to the woods until about eleven o'clock in the morning. Snowdrops were in flower in the hazel coppice, and dog's mercury was pushing up in amongst the bent green spikes of the bluebells. There was a vague promise of spring somewhere ahead and the whole group were in high spirits. They set up camp in a new area to one side of the big clearing, where levelling operations had shovelled aside a great pile of hazel stumps and made a relatively flat surface for the tents. They finished the framework and thatching of the small round house, so there was no need to have a big cook tent, and the whole camp quickly adopted a more permanent appearance. They made a camp fireplace just inside the perimeter of the settlement itself, tamped the ground smooth and laid out big ash logs to sit on. The place was beginning to look like home.

But it was a home that was frequently invaded from without. Two days a week, sometimes more, sometimes less, the camera crew were brought on to the site to record the progress of the project. On those days the hard-working volunteers were dogged by cameras and micro-phones, and asked constantly to explain what they were doing. Since the whole object of this exercise was to try and reconstruct an Iron Age environment, the presence of the camera was even more obtrusive than usual, and it took many months before the group could come to terms with it.

There were other visitors as well. Someone from the production team, Brian, Linda, most often myself, would visit every day. From time to time one or other of us would also stay the night. Quite often in the early weeks there were other experts, craftsmen of one kind or another to advise on this or that, colleagues from the BBC, local officials. But it would be wrong to give the impression that there was a constant stream of visitors. For five days a week, for twenty-two hours out of the twenty-four, the group were left entirely alone. And as time went by the place did become their home, their private place, and everyone else, including me, was there on sufferance, as a guest.

The volunteers had already begun to get themselves organised. It was agreed that each day a different couple would take a turn as cooks. They set a pattern for meal times along conventional modern lines with breakfast, lunch and dinner in the evening, a pattern that was to persist for the whole year. They also adopted a coffee break in the morning and a tea break in the afternoon, even though there was no coffee and no tea to drink. Various concoctions made with dif-ferent native herbs were tried out and in the end most people opted for a tea made from an infusion of mint or thyme and a coffee made from ground and roasted wheat. The habit was there even if the ingredients were not.

There were other modern institutions and ties with the outside world which were difficult to break. The project called for a degree of isolation which few prehistoric communities would have experienced. I was asking the group not only to break away from a modern lifestyle, but also to abandon all contact with friends and relatives. At this time it was decided that there had to be some compromise and I agreed to allow writing paper and pens one day a week and a delivery of mail from outside, so there was a quaint little ceremony every Sunday when the pens and paper were handed out and surreptitiously collected up again afterwards. This may not have helped the illusion of losing contact with the twentieth century, but it probably prevented much more severe emotional strain.

There were one or two other concessions that had deeper social effects. After much discussion we agreed that no one could be asked to risk bringing an unwanted child into the world just for the sake of a television project. Total abstinence seemed a rather unlikely prospect, so we agreed on modern contraceptives. This of course meant that the women, being free from childbirth and the risk of pregnancy, could behave as modern women and not suffer any of the restrictive penalties of motherhood, apart of course from Lindsay Ainsworth. Having compromised once we compromised twice and agreed to allow Tampax during menstruation. This again had considerable social effects. Instead of being isolated, pariahs perhaps, as many women in primitive societies are obliged to be for four or five days a month, the women were not incapacitated any more than they would have been anywhere else.

But there were still one or two minor areas of sexual discrimination. I supplied the group with a few modern tools during this first building phase. There were three modern billhooks, two bow saws and a couple of broad chisels in addition to the iron tools which were beginning to arrive on the site. The result was that there was a terrible scramble for tools every morning. The men vied with each other to demonstrate their skill and capacity for hard work. The girls, less used to building work and carpentry, found themselves left to do the dullest jobs.

I found Jill sitting on a tree stump one day, looking thoroughly irritable. 'Because we don't know how to use the tools the men don't let us have them. But if we never get to touch the tools we'll never learn! It makes me cross, so I take it out on poor old Pete. Anyway, if we go on at this rate we'll never get the place finished on time.'

The group were torn between different priorities. First there was the problem of the animals. Most were due to arrive towards the end of March, and buildings would be needed for them. Then there was the fencing – a ten-acre pasture which had to be separated, by a wattle fence, from the arable land on which the crops would be sown. Finally, or perhaps it should have been first, there was their own house, the great round house that was planned as the focal point of the whole settlement. Until it was built they had to go on living in tents, and as long as they were still in tents they still felt, as Martin put it, that they were on 'an extended camping holiday'.

But the small round house, which had almost been completed before the week's break, was now ready to have its circular walls daubed – smeared thickly with a muddy plaster to keep out the draughts. Daub itself can be made up from many different ingredients, but the basic essentials are a mixture of two parts clay and one part earth, with the addition of straw and some kind of binding material – wool or pigs' bristle – to knit the stuff together and prevent it cracking too badly when it dries out.

In the village the daub was mixed close to the well, where a large pile of clay had been dumped. The technique of daubing was not difficult, it was simply a matter of mixing together the different constituents with sufficient water to make the mixture sticky, and then carting it over to the building in progress and spreading it on the walls. Usually two people worked at once, one on the inside and one on the outside of the building, slapping the mess as hard as possible on to the wattle so that it spurted through the cracks and stuck to the layer on the other side. It was an unpleasant job. Gobs of daub would fly in all directions, coating hands, clothes and faces with a generous splatter of muck. And in March the muddy mixture was only just above freezing. Hands quickly became numb and painful by turns. Helen's hands were so cold one day that she was almost crying with the cold and Kate took time off from cooking to try and chafe some warmth into her freezing fingers. Not surprisingly, daubing was the most unpopular job of all.

'It's ridiculous,' said Sarah, wearily scraping clay off her arms. 'You spend your day pummelling daub into the ground and then digging it out again. And then having gone through this fatuous performance, you have to slap the stuff on to the walls and freeze your hands off.'

Gradually the village was beginning to take shape. The settlement itself was defined by the ditch excavated in the previous months. Later this was to be topped by a palisade of stakes and wattle fencing, but in March it was simply white, chalky soil. The main entrance faced almost due north, the shortest route to the field and the pond where the animals were watered. On the western side, just inside the surrounding bank and ditch, was the hole which was later to become the well, and then three small animal houses, the rectangular shed – at first intended for goats – the pigsty of split logs and the hen house raised on stilts to keep sleepy birds out of reach of foxes. At the southern edge, where the ground sloped slightly downwards, was the pit which was destined to become the latrine, and a couple of other deep holes in case of need. A little to the north and east of this was the little round storage house which was now complete, thatched, daubed and finished. Twenty paces north of this rose the great skeleton of the round house.

Peter Reynolds and Jack Langley had marked the positions for the thirteen oak posts which were to carry the main load of the roof, and these formed the inner ring of the house. Enclosing this inner ring was a second circle of much smaller posts which would eventually support the wall. The technique of building called for the construction of a circle of horizontal poles – the ring beam – supported by the thirteen vertical oak posts. Long rafters, some of them well over thirty feet in length, would be secured to the ring beam with their bottom ends resting on the encircling wall and the top ends raised at an angle of fifty degrees or so to form a steeply conical roof. The critical thing was the angle of the roof – too shallow and the rain would soak through the thatch, too steep and the increased expanse of the roof would call for much more thatching and the whole structure would become less stable.

All went well to begin with. The big oak posts were sunk into holes about eighteen inches deep and arranged so that the 'Y' shaped forks at the top could carry the circular ring beam. Short lengths of heavy timber laboriously cut from the surrounding woodland, most of them carrying a natural curve, were then pegged together to form the beam. The outer wall was staked and walled very quickly by the volunteers, then the first rafters were, with great labour, run up over the outer wall until they rested on the ring beam. As soon as the first two or three of these were up it was obvious that something was wrong. The angle at which they rested, instead of being a handsome fifty degrees, was more like thirty-five. Instead of a proud cone the roof looked like a squashed umbrella.

There were great post-mortems about what could possibly have gone wrong. It was obvious that the diameter of the house was too great for the height of the ring beam. Either the main supports were too short or the distance between the outer and inner rings was too great. Only a tape measure would settle the question and at this stage everybody preferred to leave it unresolved. The important thing was to put it right. But in the meantime the animals were due to arrive and the smaller buildings had to be completed without delay.

First to arrive were another batch of Soays – these from Professor Peter Jewell's research project at the Royal Holloway College in London. They were driven on to the field one bright morning by two friendly technicians from the college. The villagers built a small sheepfold of six-foot hurdles.

'You got to watch these beggars,' said the driver. 'They'll do six foot from a standing start.'

There were five ewes and a young ram, all of them less than a year old and as shy and agile as the deer in the woods. The villagers carried them one by one to the pen and watched as they huddled wildly together in one corner.

The next batch of sheep turned up a few days later. Dr Michael Ryder of the Wool Research Institute, near Edinburgh, had advised us to buy Shetlands. Dr Ryder has spent many years doing research into woollen textiles and has studied animal fibres from archaeological excavations. The structure of the wool found on a number of sites, both in Europe and in Britain, bears similarities to that of modern Shetlands. This breed frequently produces animals with brown or oatmeal coloured fleeces, but some of them are always white. It seems unlikely that the Ancient Britons had no white sheep. The classical writers describe the Britons as wearing brightly coloured garments, and it is extremely difficult to dye brown wool any colour other than brown or black. Without modern bleaching agents the only way to get bright colours is to start off with white wool. So we bought six white Shetland ewes from a farmer on the Isle of Coll, borrowed a fine Shetland ram from the Rare Breeds Survival Trust in Devon, and by mid-March had a rather peculiar little flock of sheep – seven Shetlands and eleven Soays – running around a fenced enclosure on the Iron Age farm.

Unfortunately, one of the Shetland ewes arrived with a broken leg, having had a rather rough trip in the back of a Landrover. Martin immediately took her into his care, making a splint for the leg and tying it firmly but gently into place. I held the sheep still for him while he worked, watching him anxiously. 'Do you think we ought to call a vet?' I asked him.

'Oh I think I'll manage,' he said, carefully concentrating on the injured leg.

'Are you sure,' I bleated, along with the sheep.

Martin looked at me, an expression close to exasperation in his eyes. 'Look, if I can't manage with a blinking sheep, what do you think will happen if one of us breaks a leg?'

He had a point. I shut up and hung silently on to the sheep while he finished tying on the splint. Soon the injured ewe was tottering along on four legs again.

On the twenty-first of March the first goat arrived. Shandy was a gentle, honey-coloured creature with liquid brown eyes and horns like an Iron Age lyre. The villagers were delighted to see her. Sharon made her a collar of macramé and put her to bed in the pigsty because the goat shed was not yet finished. Over the next few days Shandy was joined by several more goats, all with splendid horns, and most of them with coats of many colours. Some of them were borrowed from loving owners and others were bought outright. There was little Sula, re-christened Lucy, a tiny half-wild nanny from the island of Skokholm off the Welsh coast. She was small and neat, with a tiny udder, perhaps the nearest thing to an Ancient British goat that one could find today, but it was one of Lucy's byre mates who really looked the part, the amazing Shaggy Maggy – a huge, hirsute creature from Ireland with enormous horns, eyes as big as those of a Jersey cow, and a devout belief in her own humanity. She associated with the other goats as little as possible, always choosing to be with human beings, even if she had to butt them severely in order to make them aware of her presence. She had a turbulent history, having been rescued from an Irish knackers' yard, to become the much indulged pet of a wealthy Anglo-Irish family. The confusion of mind which such a varied background had produced was stamped indelibly on Maggy's character. She gave very little milk and caused more trouble than all the other goats put together, but the village would not have been the same without her.

Two other nannies arrived shortly after Shandy. One of them was in such a hurry to give birth that she produced one kid in the Landrover on her way to the village and the other within minutes of her arrival. These were joined shortly afterwards by a Dexter cow and calf from Joe Henson's Cotswold Farm Park in Gloucestershire, fourteen assorted barnyard chickens and, most important of all, the pigs.

At Peter Reynolds' request some months before, Joe Henson had mated a completely intractable wild boar to a couple of Tamworth sows. Tamworths, with their shaggy red coats and long snouts, are the most primitive-looking breed to survive the improvements of the last couple of hundred years. The progeny of the two sows, bursting with hybrid vigour, turned out twice the size of father and just as nasty. But Joe, not to be deterred, crossed the savage offspring with one another, carefully selecting the least homicidal of both sexes. The resulting crossbreeds, two generations later, still looked like wild boars (with rather fat behinds – a desirable trait for those who like roast pork) but possessed of the temperament of normal, benign farmyard pigs. That, anyway, is what Joe had said.

Idi the boar and two sturdy gilts, later named Gudrun and Goldie, arrived in a trailer at the field's edge. From the unloading point there were still two or three hundred yards of woodland and muddy clearing before the safety of their log sty. The problem was to convey these large and energetic creatures, which were in a state of tumultuous alarm after their journey, from the trailer to the sty without mishap. John Rockliff was full of ideas as he calmly surveyed the big boar, while it charged like a tank at the trailer door.

'I think he's quite tame,' he said optimistically. 'Let's put a string round his middle and another round one leg and sort of lead him over.'

'What about hurdles?' said Martin. 'Couldn't we walk him along with hurdles all around him?'

'It would take for ever,' said somebody else.

'I think he'll be all right,' John insisted. 'Let's give it a try.'

Suiting his actions to his words, John climbed on board the trailer and scrambled around, falling over pigs and tangling himself with string as he and Martin fought to get it connected to Idi's massive frame.

'OK, let the door down,' yelled John.

As soon as the ramp was down three hundredweight of terrified pork hurtled down it with John dragged behind like an old shoe tagged on to a newlyweds' getaway car. The camera team and a group of would-be swine herds scattered in all directions, and in a trail of broken string Idi the pig burst free and took to the woods, obviously intent on becoming the first free wild boar in Britain for three hundred years.

Everybody, including the film unit, followed in ragged pursuit, crashing into trees and stumbling over stumps in an effort to keep Idi in view. Fortunately, the forest is neutral. Idi, too, found his progress impeded by the undergrowth and within a minute or two his trailing cords were tangled up in a patch of bramble. He stopped in bewilderment, uncertain which way to turn. I could see that if he were to make a determined effort he could easily snap the cord again and take off deeper into the woods, so we formed a ring around him, gently closing in and whispering quiet endearments. With so many people around him he still hesitated, unsure where to run. At last I was close enough to creep softly up behind him, reaching forward with infinite caution to try and grasp his powerful hocks.

'What's the plan?' murmured Brian.

'As soon as I catch his legs, everybody jump on him,' I hissed, and a second later my hands closed on his back legs.

In an instant there was pandemonium. With incredible power and agility for one so portly, Idi somersaulted over on top of me, all but tearing his legs from my grasp as the rest of the hunters pounced. Squashed underneath a writhing mass of muscle and fat I felt like the loser in a catchweight wrestling contest. But the worst thing was the noise, scream after piggy scream of rage, terror and anguish, blowing out the eardrums of everyone within a hundred yards of him and sending distant echoes to the furthest reaches of the forest. Tom, the film sound recordist, who had stood by his guns as it were, watched in dumbfounded disbelief as the needle on his tape recorder jolted into the red and almost disappeared off the dial. I still wonder why, in all those fulsome accounts of boar hunts which abound in ancient myth and legend, no chronicles ever mention the screams raised to heaven by the unlucky trophy of the day.

With six or seven healthy human beings sitting on him and, incidentally, on me, even Idi's enormous strength was of no avail. At last somebody brought a hurdle and Idi was tied down on top of it and carried, ceremonially, to his new home. It took ten people, all puffing a bit, to carry him the three hundred yards to the pig pen, but once inside the sturdy log enclosure, with all obvious escape routes blocked, Idi seemed to settle down. Within minutes he was quietly snuffling around the sty and after a few days John Rockliff, chief pig keeper for the time being, was able to climb into the pen with him and scratch his back, to the evident enjoyment of both of them. Idi eventually became extraordinarily tame, quite happy to wander quietly around the compound like some gigantic overweight lap dog. But his quiet and modest demeanour betrayed in him a want of that aggressive masculinity which is a necessary requirement for a wild boar. The two gilts, Goldie and Gudrun, his constant companions day and night, came in and went out of season unloved and unregarded. The group's efforts over the following months to arouse his interest in the female pigs and to help him follow it up in a positive way would fill a small book on the more bizarre aspects of pig keeping. But all this was in the future.

The complete complement of animals on the Iron Age ark to begin with was as follows: five Dexter cattle, four cows and a steer calf, nine nanny goats, almost all of them in kid, thirty-two chickens, most of them Old English Game, six geese, and eighteen sheep, eleven Soays and seven Shetlands. Four of the Soays were rams, three of which were clearly destined for the table and most of the ewes were very pregnant. Then there were the two dogs, Sirius, a pretty little lurcher bitch who was to pay her way with rabbits and hares for the table, and Emer, a large and shaggy mongrel with a threatening bark and a lovable disposition. Sirius, of course, took her name from the Roman dog star, but she was always called Siri, for short. Emer, more Celtic, was named after the wife of the great Irish hero of the myths, Cuchulain.

Throughout these first few weeks the group were still living in tents. Even with straw tucked underneath the groundsheets the flimsy nylon walls offered little protection against the driving rain and bitter winds of that late, cold spring. To make matters worse the plastic zips burst on most of the tents so that the wind billowed the canopies like tattered balloons. The camp site took on the character of a refugee camp after a particularly nasty natural disaster. Cardboard boxes and empty cans littered the muddy ground and the gaudy colours of the tents seemed like a sick joke contrived by a malicious manufacturer to jeer at the mud-soaked surroundings.

In the evenings the whole group crowded round the cook's fire. This was in the centre of a square arrangement of newly-felled ash poles which made convenient seats, and faces and fronts got nicely roasted in the fire. Backs, especially that gap between sweater and jeans, got well chilled by the evening air. Everyone had chilblains and spent hours comparing them with other people's for size and viciousness.

On wet nights the group crammed themselves into the one small round house which was now more or less complete. There was a smelly paraffin stove in the middle which scarcely took the chill off and was hopelessly inadequate for drying clothes. They tried lighting a fire instead, but the tiny hut quickly filled with choking smoke and they were obliged to go back to the oil heater. Clothes were permanently damp, and began to smell of mildew. In the day time people would take time off from building to have a quick warm up by the cook's fire, but there was nowhere really warm, nowhere comfortable. The pressure was on to get the big round house built.

Chapter Four

At the beginning of April the roof still looked like the rusted spikes of some giant skeletal umbrella. Either the overall diameter of the building had to be reduced or the level of the ring beam had to be raised so that the pitch of the roof could be increased. The group had already tried to raise the angle of the rafters by laboriously re-cutting the mortise and tenon joints lower down on the wall posts which had the effect of tipping the rafters up at a steeper angle, but the alteration was not big enough. The only alternative was to increase the height of the ring beam by placing a second circle of horizontal timbers above the first.

One by one John Rossetti and Brian raised additional logs above the ring beam and pegged them into position. The circle of timbers then assumed a rather odd appearance, with a succession of shallow triangular humps running all round the circumference, rather like a ring of mating hippos, as Martin observed. But it worked. New rafters, freshly cut from the surrounding woods, were hauled to the site and slowly raised over the outside wall, up to the highest level of the switchback ring beam and on up to the apex where the longest of them came together in uncertain conjunction at the top. Pete Ainsworth and John Rossetti, each shinning up a separate rafter, met in wobbly mid-air to join the main poles together at the top in a tangle of tight lashed cord. The peak of the roof was still far from being a perfect cone, but it was a big improvement on what had gone before.

Felling the young trees for the rafters – mostly ash and birch poles – dragging them through the woods and then pushing them up on to the skeleton roof was an enormous labour. It took six or eight people, both men and women, to carry the heavy poles, short ones in the front, taller people at the rear, bumping and shuffling through the woods like a giant disabled centipede.

'All these short men,' said Sharon acidly. 'Some of the tall girls here have to do all the work.'

Somehow, despite the bumps and bruises and wearing effort, they succeeded in mounting seventy-four rafters on the roof, some reaching

Thatching the round house, towards the end of April before 'going
Iron Age'. The ladder on the left is modern.

only as far as the main ring beam, some rising to a second, higher,
ring about eight feet short of the apex, and a few going all the way up
to meet at the peak of the great cone.

As soon as the rafters were in place there was a great mixing and
slapping on of daub around the low circular wall of the house. Meanwhile, the thatch began to creep slowly up the lower flanks. Thatching
on the smaller animal houses had all been done by the laborious
technique of tying on tight bundles of straw, but faced with the daunting expanse of the great round house roof the group were in need of a
more rapid and efficient technique. A couple of professional thatchers
were called in and they demonstrated how to lay a 'dressing' layer of
loose straw on top of the battens.

The first team of thatchers would move slowly round the perimeter
of the roof, one throwing up bundles of straw, the other laying them
on top of the dressing layer, battering the ends smooth with a notched
wooden paddle, known as a leggatt, and then securing them with pegs
and heavy planks of wood. Behind the first team of two came the
sewing team. One clung to the roof on the outside, one perched on a
fragile support on the inside and they passed a big wooden 'needle'

Brian beating up the thatch on the goat byre with a leggatt. The pigsty is in the background.

through the thatch, tying on the outside, pulling tight on the inside. Usually, though not always, the thatchers who did the sewing were both men, the advance team with the bundles, women.

Thatching was not just extremely hard, blistering work. It was also extremely hazardous. Once a thatcher lost his or her tenuous perch on the roof a fall of some kind was inevitable. Kate lost her footing on the outside once and went slithering down the steep thatch like a riderless toboggan. Fortunately, she was shaken but not hurt. Pete Little twice fell off the fragile inner support and both times miraculously escaped injury. The group seemed remarkably cheerful at the risks involved, but I lived in daily terror of some ghastly accident.

Despite my admiration for their achievements, it sometimes seemed to me that their work rate was dismally slow, and that it took them a long time every day to sort out who was to do what. Those who believe in the virtues of leadership would maintain that this was inevitable as long as there was no one around to give them clear, concise orders. I had always felt that it was necessary for them to work out their own problems if they were going to survive the year as a cohesive group. But I did occasionally allow myself the luxury of a few words of advice and, even more occasionally, a few mild criticisms. After I had com-

The village in May, with the bank and ditch in the foreground. This
was later topped with a palisade. The new goat house is in the centre,
the small round house on the right, the round house at the back.

mented, perhaps rather reproachfully, on their slow rate of progress
one day, I found myself face to face with Kate. Her round, normally
good-natured face was pink with indignation.

'Look,' she said, 'you're doing an experiment to see if it's possible for
us to work in an Iron Age way on an Iron Age project.' She glared at
me out of saucer blue eyes. 'Well, you've done your experiment and it
isn't!' And she flounced back to resume thatching the roof.

Of course she was right. There was no way that this group of young
people could break the social patterns they had grown up with,
abandon all the roles and institutions they were accustomed to. The
aim of the project was not to try and recreate Iron Age people, but to
see whether modern people could adapt to Iron Age conditions. So it
was interesting to see how the Ainsworth children, without developed
prejudices of their own, would react to their surroundings.

During the colder weather Lindsay was worried about Robin, the
three-year-old, who seemed miserable. He was bewildered by the cold
biting into his fingers, and spent much of the time in tears. He also
had a lot of difficulty keeping his meal time bread and stew out of the
reach of the dogs and thieving chickens. But the older boys, Peter and
Nick, seemed to find inexhaustible entertainment around the site.

They would pick up the tools – axes, saws, heavy mallets – and attempt to use them in happy imitation of their elders. It was terrifying to watch an axe burying its shining edge between little pink fingers or a hammer narrowly missing a childish head. Miraculously there were no accidents and the children busied themselves building a tiny round house, a slightly rickety miniature version of the great round shape which now rose, half complete, at the northern end of the compound.

Little Peter Ainsworth and Nick also constructed an elaborate cage of twigs and string in a small clearing in the woods. It had a ramshackle door with a primitive arrangement of strings and triggers which was intended to click shut on any unfortunate animal or bird that should venture inside in pursuit of the scattered grain bait. The obvious target birds were pheasants, but pheasants, in the much used but rather ugly phrase of the project, are very 'un-Iron Age'. They are native to the Far East, not the forests of England, and most of them had been born and bred in cages. Unlikely though it was that the boys would catch one of these simple minded birds, I still thought I had better take the heavy line of authority.

'You know you're not allowed to catch pheasants don't you?' I glared at Nick. He turned on me such a look of contrived innocence that I found it difficult not to laugh, but his brother came to the rescue.

'It's for rabbits,' he said firmly, then remembering that rabbits also were not entirely in period for prehistoric Britain, he added, 'or hares.'

But the children's formal education also had to be organised. By prior arrangement two people from the Education Authority, a man and a woman, turned up at the site one day. Dressed in dark suits, they sat primly on the edge of a log, while Lindsay and Peter Ainsworth debated with them about the children's educational needs.

'Don't they both look *clean*,' hissed Sarah in a whisper.

Fortunately, authority was possessed of a sense of proportion. It was agreed that the children could be taught on the settlement, making use of the combined educational qualifications of Jill, Sarah and Kate. Slates and chalks, later replaced by exercise books, were brought on to the site and Pete and Nick received the rudiments of the three R's for an hour or two every day. Far from falling behind their schoolmates, they both seemed to make splendid progress.

There was one other invasion from outside before contact with the world could be broken off, and this was a press conference. For this occasion the group put on their Iron Age clothes for the first time. The

Very 'un-Iron Age' books for the boys' education. Sarah is working with Nick and Peter Ainsworth.

clothes were made by the BBC wardrobe department under the guidance of Dr Anne Ross, of Southampton University. Dr Ross had shown us photographs of numerous classical statues representing defeated Celtic warriors, usually in the act of being executed by the Romans. There are also a number of ancient references to Celtic clothing, and a few garments have survived intact in the Danish peat bogs. Using an amalgam of all this material the designer had produced a male costume consisting of baggy trousers, a short smock belted at the waist, a sheepskin waistcoat and a long cloak. All the garments were wool except for shirts and underpants of linen. Most of the fabric was homespun, and bright with checks and tartans, the designs mentioned in ancient literature and borne out by the surviving fragments of cloth.

The women's dress consisted of long skirts with separate smock tops, long woollen overdresses and long cloaks like the men's. Some of these garments were not quite as becoming as they might have been. Kate's brown dress gave her a slightly monkish look. 'Friar Tuck' crowed the other girls, and the name stuck. Some of the men also had a rather odd appearance, like refugee children provided with secondhand clothes by a well meaning but short-sighted relief worker.

When the reporters and cameramen of the press arrived on the site on a blustery day in late April, the general flavour of a disaster zone was accentuated by the unfinished round house, amid the muddy slough of the compound. Press men in clean shoes picked their way delicately about, asking pertinent questions. 'What happens if one of the girls gets pregnant?' 'Have you got a television?' 'Where's the nearest pub?'

They crowded the site all through one interminable morning, posing the more photogenic villagers against convincing Iron Age backdrops. When at last they had all gone the group collapsed, disappearing to the tents and not emerging for the rest of the day. Sarah had a violent migraine, the first for many weeks. No amount of toil in the mud and cold had produced such total exhaustion.

The following day, in heavy rain, they got back to work again. Morale was not very good, but the animals helped people to take their minds off their own problems. The goats had by this time produced six kids, four nannies and two billies, but one of the nanny kids was a pathetic undersized creature with little stumpy legs which seemed unequal to the task of supporting the tiny body. It expired, to everybody's sadness, a day or two later. Out in the field the first of the Shetland lambs were also born and one of them, inevitably a ewe lamb, was also in a bad way. It seemed to be paralysed in its back legs and was unable to raise itself high enough to reach the teat. The mother ewe, with that harsh instinct which humans find so hard to bear, nursed its twin and abandoned the weakling to lie bleating feebly on the short, cold grass. Martin picked up the pathetic little creature, placed it in a warm basket and took it inside the small round house, but despite his best efforts and the help of a very twentieth-century feeding bottle, it, too, expired. Martin was more successful with the ewe with the broken leg, now christened Elizabeth. He had secured her in a little separate hurdle enclosure of her own so that she could not rush around too much and break her leg all over again. Under his care, the leg mended well.

The grass in the field was late growing and the round house was slow to rise, but it had been agreed long before that May the first was D-day for going 'Iron Age'. On that date everyone was determined to get rid of their blue jeans and sweaters, don their Celtic garments and abandon the tents, tin cans, plastic bowls and general clutter of the modern camp site. They would move into the round house and scrape the mud of the twentieth century off their feet. But when I came down to the site on April the thirtieth I was appalled to see that there was still an enormous gaping hole in the roof of the round house. And the weather looked even less promising than usual.

'Look, I just can't do it to you,' I said to the group. 'Your sheepskin rugs will be soaking wet in ten minutes if it comes on to rain. Let's hang on to the tents for a bit longer and postpone the move until the roof's finished.'

This helpful suggestion was received in non-committal silence. 'We'll talk about it,' was all the volunteers would say.

As soon as the film unit had retired from the scene they had a long discussion about whether to abandon the tents and other modern gear or keep them for another couple of weeks. By all accounts it was a fairly heated argument and when they came to take a vote on it the cook of the day, who was obliged to act as chairperson, had to give the casting vote. They decided to go ahead. It was their first completely independent decision and the beginning of a new collective autonomy for the group.

So on May eve, with the Celtic festival of Beltain to mark the beginning of a new phase of the project, the tents were rolled up and packed away, clothes bundled up and loaded on to a van to be washed and stored, tools and tin cans were taken away and the clearing in the forest cleansed of twentieth-century litter.

Before they went to bed they all went out into the woods to cut a may pole in preparation for the following day's festivities. It was a beautiful straight young silver birch with a flourish of pale green leaves at the top. Each person in turn took a cut with the axe until Helen finally brought it to the ground. They carried the young tree ceremonially to the home clearing. They then doused the fire in the old outside cooking place which had served them while they were living in tents. The new fire, lit specially for Beltain in accordance with old Celtic custom, would be in the centre of the round house.

The group slept that night in their sheepskin rugs, cosily arranged on heaps of hay under the sheltering ridge of thatch above the curving west wall of the great round house. And though it rained during the night their sheepskins were still dry in the morning.

Chapter Five

Beltain is one of the most important days in the ancient Celtic calendar. There are four principal festivals at three-month intervals throughout the year and all have survived into modern times in slightly different guises. Lugnasa, on August the first, is still with us in the great British festival of August Bank Holiday, a time for fun and games. Samhain, the dark festival of oncoming winter, traditionally celebrated on October the thirty-first, survives in the Church calendar as All-Hallows Eve, but is more vigorously remembered in Britain on Bonfire Night. Imbolc, at the beginning of February, is still celebrated in the Catholic Church, especially in Ireland, as St Brigid's day. Brig, or Brigga, was a goddess throughout the Celtic world many centuries before she was sanctified by the Christian Church. In England it is possible that the festival has jumped a little with the Gregorian calendar to St Valentine's Day. But Beltain, May Day, is perhaps the most flourishing of all the ancient festivals today, celebrated as it is with special emphasis by Marxist-Leninist regimes in all parts of the world who have never heard of the Celts and would not care if they had.

Beltain was a time for sacrifice, almost certainly human sacrifice. It was the time when the flocks were blessed and purified in expectation of the spring crop of young animals, and it was also a useful date for moving the cattle and sheep from their winter quarters to the summer pastures, where the grass would be beginning to grow lush and strong. The group were determined to celebrate the beginning of their new life in style.

Very early in the morning, before sunrise, they all got up and walked through the woods, carrying with them a breakfast picnic of bread and butter, hard boiled eggs and honey. The children wailed a bit at being hauled out of their beds at such an unreasonable hour into the chill of a dark and misty morning. Jill had been elected May Queen the day before because, as she explained to me, 'they all know I'm dying to get pregnant so they're making me the fertility figure.'

She was obviously both amused and touched by the compliment, so it was Jill who led the way in the half light through the woods until they came to a clearing where they could face the sunrise to the east.

The morning mist hung between the trees, leaving tiny beads of moisture on their rough woollen clothes. Acres of half open bluebells, stretching as far as the eye could see across the forest floor, glowed in the half light, a great lake of milky blue. Lindsay, seeking to get in tune with the Celtic mysteries, entered her own spiritual domain and sank to the grass for a brief session of Yoga exercises. As the sun rose slowly, an orange haze in the east, they all stood quietly in mute contemplation of a new dawn.

Spring euphoria then seems to have taken over. They returned to the home field and one by one, Jill taking the lead as befitted the fertility symbol of the day, they took off their clothes, rolled in the dew soaked grass and wandered about naked in the chilly morning air. Only Brian and Pete Ainsworth refused to join in the naked pagan rites. Pete was unapologetic.

'I felt that it was up to the two eldest males to stand ready to defend the rest against evil spirits, because evil spirits really get to you when you're naked. Anyway,' he added, 'it was too bloody cold to take my clothes off.'

Their early morning exertions proved too much for most of them and they returned to the warmth of their sheepskin rugs and went back to sleep again. By the time the film crew arrived at about ten o'clock the day was just beginning all over again.

All the girls picked garlands of primroses and bluebells to wear in their hair. They gathered fresh young branches to decorate the door-ways of their new home, but when they came to check the Maypole they found the glorious crown of pale green leaves which had adorned its top was now an ugly skeleton of stripped wintry twigs. The goats had got to the Maypole before them. All day the goats continued to celebrate in their own way, happily removing decorations and digesting them. Fortunately nobody minded very much. It was, after all, a day to be enjoyed.

But there was, as with all celebrations, a fair amount of hard work that had gone before in order to ensure the success of the day. Martin had spent hour after hour grinding flour on the quern in order to bake a special Beltain bannock, a cake which was rumoured to contain secret ingredients. This Beltain bannock was also a part of the Celtic lore. In ancient times, Dr Ross had assured the group, the Beltain cake always emerged from the oven with one portion marked with a mysterious burn. The bannock was divided up among the young men and maidens of the community, and the person who received the burnt portion was marked down as the sacrificial victim. In earliest times the sacrifice would of course have been final, but in rituals which survived into the present century, the sentence had been commuted to something less drastic, a ducking, a forfeit, a tiny flicker of a gesture to the old gods. Martin prepared his bannock with great care and marked it with radial lines, dividing it evenly into sixteen portions, one more than was strictly necessary. With half the settlement looking on he then placed it in the pit oven he had prepared, with a healthy glow of live charcoal in the bottom, and left it to bake. But when he came to remove it, some hours later, he found to his amazement – or so he still strenuously maintains – that on one point of the bannock's rim there was a mysterious circular burn, about the size of a tenpenny piece.

This manifestation of the dark powers produced as many different reactions as there were people in the group, but its presence filled some with unspoken, half embarrassed alarm. Any suggestion of chucking the whole thing into the fire deeply offended Martin who had spent so many hours baking the day before. So it was decided to have a formal discussion to decide the bannock's fate.

Everything stopped while the whole group gathered in the hollow square of ash logs around the cooking fire. The debate that was then recorded on film was typical of many of the discussions that preceded each moment of collective decision. The group were all very close together in age. Most of them had very decided views and strong personalities, otherwise they would never have volunteered in the first place. And they were all brought up in that liberal democratic tradition that has everything to do with the second half of the twentieth century and nothing at all to do with the Iron Age. The result was that all major decisions took up a great amount of time while everyone put their point. But, except for certain important issues like whether or not to move into the unfinished round house, decisions rarely had to be put to the vote. They simply talked the matter through until everyone had had a say.

The debate dragged on for what seemed like hours, but at last a compromise solution was found. It was agreed that the cake should be broken up into small pieces and placed into two bowls. One bowl, the one on the right, contained only guaranteed unburnt fragments. The burnt piece, along with several others, was put in the bowl on the left. Both bowls were then placed inside the little round house and people went in one by one to take the portion of their choice, so that no one would witness the private moment of confrontation with the powers of evil.

However, the honour of the whole community was saved by Pete Little, who went boldly to the left-hand bowl, seized the offending lump of burnt cake and began to eat it before anybody had a chance to start arguing again.

'What are we going to do with him then?' asked Martin.

'Duck him in the pond,' suggested somebody unkindly.

'Make him run the gauntlet.'

This suggestion was quickly taken up and people ran to cut hazel switches from the nearby bushes. Pete had his mouth too full of cake to protest. Jill, who might have been expected to have Pete's welfare most at heart, selected a hazel bough for herself and then busied herself tearing off others for the children. 'Come on Robin,' she said cheerfully, 'we're all going to hit Pete.'

The whole group lined up in two files, facing one another. Pete, clutching his woolly cap to his head with one hand and still stuffing cake into his mouth with the other, ran furiously between the lines while the hazel twigs slapped against his shoulders. He reached the end and turned.

'Hey, how many times do I have to do this?' he complained, through a mouthful of cake.

'Seven,' said Sharon, remorselessly.

It seemed the right kind of ritual number.

So seven times Pete ran between the lines of hazel branches. Perhaps it was just as well that most of the blows just brushed him lightly or missed altogether. All the same, it was noticeable that some of the branches looked decidedly frayed at the end of the seventh run.

It was a very minor act of exorcism. And, for most people, a bit of a giggle.

The more serious act of sacrifice was the first killing on the project, the execution of a young Soay ram. There had been much discussion the night before about who should do the killing and exactly how it should be done. Everyone looked to Martin as he had taken on the job of looking after the sheep, nursing the sick lambs and getting the injured ewe on her feet again. If he knew how to save life, ran the curious logic, he ought also to know how to take it. It was not a job that Martin relished, but he thought he ought to do it.

'After all,' he told me later, 'if you're going to eat meat you've got to be prepared to kill for it. Otherwise, you're just ducking the issue.'

46

The ram was caught and brought to a tree on the edge of the wood. A line was thrown over a bough, so that the sheep could be hauled up for butchering. While John Rossetti and John Rockliff held the beast still, Martin took one of the big fencing mallets and struck it heavily between the eyes. As the blow fell the ram staggered and sank to its knees. They hauled it up by its legs and Martin stabbed deeply into its throat. There was a convulsion as the blood poured out and then the ram was still. The whole thing was over in seconds, but for most of the villagers it was the first time they had ever killed.

The ram was butchered by Helen and Sarah, both with their Beltain coronets of flowers still on their heads as they wielded the bloody knife. Then it was skewered, more or less expertly, on a wooden spit, to be roasted over the fire, but the Beltain fire was giving problems. According to custom the fire had to be lit anew for the festival and the group had extinguished their fire the night before. But how were they to light the new one? They had practised vigorously with a fire drill, a simple mechanism consisting of a horizontal piece of wood for a hearth, a vertical rod for the drill, a bow with a loose string looped around the drill and a bearing at the top made of a little wooden cup greased with lard. One person presses down on the bearing, driving the drill into the hearth, while the other vigorously saws away with the bow. Within the first few seconds the drill wears away a little depression in the hearth. Within a minute or less there is a strong smell of scorching and, with luck and a great deal of effort, a thin plume of woodsmoke. Theoretically, or so all the books on the subject cheerfully maintain, the sawdust in the drill hole then ignites and can be transferred to a tinder of dry hay or wood shavings. Armed with all this information Pete Little sawed away at the fire drill. And sawed. And sawed. After half an hour he was ready to give up.

'I think there's more smoke under my armpits than there is in that firedrill,' he observed.

'I've seen Australian Aborigines do it in thirty seconds,' said Sarah, unhelpfully.

Fortunately, there was a friendly tribe of film cameramen with a cigarette lighter on hand to kindle the Beltain fire.

Later in the day, with two fires burning brightly in the entrance gateway and a third with the spitted ram roasting nicely over it, the group set about driving their flocks through the smoke in order to purify them and ensure fertility for the coming year. This is one of the few rituals which is well attested by the ancient authors and it appealed to the villagers as one which they could perform without feeling too foolish. However, the idea of driving all the cows and the entire flock of sheep through fire and smoke was a little daunting. Instead, they decided to take one representative of each species between the fires in the hope that the benefits conferred on one beast might somehow be imparted to the others.

Lindsay led Mary, the old Dexter, through the smoke without incident, except that at times it seemed that the cow was leading Lindsay. Brian battled through with the black nanny goat, Annabelle. Then it was Idi's turn. Everybody had vivid memories of trying to take Idi for a walk, so, with more faith in his homing instinct than I would have been able to muster, they decided to drive the boar between the fires and hope he would come back again. I watched with alarm as the great pig trundled out of his sty, lurched uncertainly towards the smoky fires, then, stamping in alarm, bolted between them and ran off into the clearing beyond. Goodbye Idi, I thought and then relapsed into gloomy imaginings of confrontations with outraged owners of distant vegetable gardens and ravaged fields. But Idi did not go far. He ran in a wide circle round the clearing and without pause, still running, headed straight back between the fires again and back into the compound. For him, as for the whole group, it was already home.

Chapter Six

Now that the group had moved in they became for the first time the proper inhabitants of the village which they themselves had built. Although I still thought of them as 'the volunteers' they were now entitled to be spoken of as villagers in their own right. They were already almost completely self-sufficient, because they had been supplied with enough food and clothing to carry them through the next four months, a kind of bank roll of stores which was meant to represent the accumulated winter supplies of an Iron Age community. The stored food and some of the other commodities were in their raw state, and for the first four weeks the group had great difficulty catering for the simplest necessities of life. Wheat, for instance, had to be ground into flour on a stone hand mill, or quern, before it could be baked. And raw wool had to be spun on a hand spindle before it could be used as thread for making clothes. From now onwards tasks like these became the daily chores of the villagers, but they were also ready to take up the agricultural work which had been set aside while they were occupied with building.

Because of the tight schedule, some of the crops had been drilled by machine before the project started. There were about two acres of wheat – a modern spring variety because there was no chance of getting enough of the ancient species wheats – an acre of barley and the same of oats and a little over half an acre each of peas and beans. Celtic beans, still called 'tic' beans and grown as cattle feed in parts of Britain, were one of the great staples of Iron Age diet. Peas were widely grown in most of Europe during prehistoric times, but whether or not they were an established crop in Iron Age Britain is still uncertain. On the remaining acre of land the villagers raised a quantity of other vegetables which are known to have been grown for thousands of years. These included wild parsnips, which still grow abundantly on the slopes below many Celtic hill forts, fat hen – a nourishing weed that tastes like spinach – leeks, linseed or flax, white mustard and charlock, both of which have leaves which taste like cabbage. In a little fenced enclosure close to the palisade they also grew herbs –

mint, thyme, marjoram, comfrey – and also woad – the blue dye plant which Julius Caesar described as the Britons' favourite colouring agent. Unfortunately the wild deer and the only slightly less wild goats broke into this enclosure and destroyed almost everything, including some carefully nurtured black currant bushes. But all the plants which the animals had spared were now bursting with leaf and would soon be clogged with weeds. Some labour had to be spared to till the land and care for the animals.

The six Shetland ewes had produced nine lambs between them. They had actually given birth to twelve lambs in all, but three had died or been stillborn, perhaps because of the rather rough handling the mother ewes had received when they first arrived. The little Soay ewes lambed about a fortnight later than the Shetlands and produced only a single offspring apiece, three male and one female. Martin tended the sheep with loving attention, taking them water in stave buckets and preventing the cattle from stealing their feed. The captive ewe with the broken leg produced her twin lambs, both rams. Since she bore the name of Elizabeth the two lambs were inevitably christened Charles and Andrew. Celtic awareness did not always descend to the naming of names.

All the goat kids were also named as soon as they were born. Peggy, a sturdy little goat with a coat the colour of milky coffee, had two kids on May morning which were promptly dubbed Beltain and May. Nina, the big white nanny, had a single white kid amongst the bluebells in the wood, and this babe in the woods, a female, was christened Persephone by Sharon before it had a chance to run away. Lucy, the little wild goat from Skokholm, produced two nanny kids with pretty marbled markings. Unfortunately, one got caught in the rain and shortly afterwards died of pneumonia. Despite having only a tiny udder Lucy was a very good mother, unlike Annabelle, who had a handsome nanny kid which she neglected, butting it away from her bulging teats, even though she had milk to spare. So Lucy took on Annabelle's baby in place of the kid that died. The little creature spent all day long with her foster mother so as to be around at feeding time, and then spent her nights curled up alongside Annabelle. The arrangement seemed to work out to the complete satisfaction of all the parties concerned. In all, fourteen kids were born to the nine nannies in the village, only three of which were males. Because the project was only for a year and there was no pressing need to build up a flock, all the kids were taken off the site and sold to eager buyers: the proceeds were then turned, with the help of the production team, into honey,

Sarah bringing in the goats for milking. Easter is in the lead and Shaggy Maggy in the foreground.

salt and beer, which were always in short supply in the settlement. This 'trading', which developed into quite a lively little exchange of commodities (the villagers even swapped bread for butter and eggs during a strike by the baker's union), was a reasonable mechanism for getting rid of surplus produce. Iron Age Celts went in for the same kind of thing, trading products as diverse as iron bars and hunting dogs the length and breadth of Europe. As far as the sale of the kids was concerned, the exchange also had the advantage of enabling the group to consume all the goats' milk themselves.

Lactic cheese was a staple item in the villagers' diet and the cows were still not producing any milk, since they were not due to calve until much later in the year. One of the Dexters, a pathetic little creature called Brigid, had arrived in very poor condition. She still had not completely weaned a bouncing six-month-old steer calf and it looked as though the strain of feeding him through the winter had told heavily on her. To make matters worse she was badly infected with warbles, a curiously nasty parasitic fly. The adult warble lays its eggs on the cow's forequarters during the summer. In the course of grooming itself the animal licks off some of the eggs and swallows them. In the cow's stomach they hatch out into maggots which slowly eat their

Mary the Dexter cow, with Helen and Martin. Mary has a macramé collar, Helen and Martin are wearing the 'Iron Age' clothes produced by the BBC wardrobe department.

way out, tunnelling through the wretched beast's flesh like woodworms in an old floorboard. Finally they end up just beneath the surface of the skin, usually along the ridge of the spine, where they form little bumps, like blind boils, but which on close inspection reveal a small air passage the size of a pin prick through which the maggot breathes. Left to itself the larva in due course pupates into a chrysalis and eventually emerges as a full blown warble fly, ready to start the whole disgusting life cycle all over again.

Pete Ainsworth spotted the warble bumps along poor Brigid's back quite early on, but lacking any modern pesticide he hesitated to take any action, as the warble boils easily become infected. Eventually, unable to bear the poor beast's suffering, he and Pete Little decided to see what they could do. With a lot of coaxing and a great deal of physical effort they secured Brigid in a primitive 'crush', a heavily staked enclosure where she could be tied up tight with no room to thrash about. They then felt gently through the rough hair on her back until they located each bump with its maggot tenant. A deft squeeze and the maggot popped out to face execution on a nearby fence post. Brigid bore the operation patiently as they squeezed out each worm in turn, taking great care to extract the whole parasite in order to avoid the danger of infection. They took out twenty-four warbles altogether and as soon as they were gone Brigid began to recover. With the fresh new grass in the field she was soon quite plump again and her black coat, which had looked grey and dusty, took on a shiny black gloss.

The goats, too, had their share of parasites. One or two of them, perhaps those from deprived homes, had arrived with lice, and these quickly transferred to the kids, clustering thickly around their heads and little bare abdomens like whole galaxies of tiny mobile warts. These unpleasant little visitors showed only a sporadic taste for human blood, but the ticks were less discriminating. The goats picked them up in the long grass and undergrowth around the settlement. Before long there was hardly anyone in the village who had not found one of these creatures clinging to his or her skin, like a small malevolent black fruit. A sharp tug and the tick would release its grasp to be squashed deftly between finger and thumb, ejecting a blackish squirt of freshly sucked blood in its death throes. Lindsay was horrified to find large numbers of them on the children, but the boys themselves were not particularly worried.

'I like squashing them,' said Pete, zestfully, as he mashed a couple of ticks on top of a fence post.

For a long time everyone wondered where all the ticks came from, but later on, when a freshly killed deer was brought into the village, it too was found to be hung about with them. Clearly ticks were literally inseparable from the whole way of life.

Whatever the snags of animal husbandry, everybody enjoyed working with the livestock. It made a welcome change from the endless labour of building. The only animal that remained unresponsive, at least to others of his own kind, was Idi the boar, who still resolutely refused to get the message of spring. Seeing their chances of a litter of piglets diminishing with every missed opportunity on Idi's part, the pig keepers, John Rockliff and Jill, began to look at Idi in a new light.

'I'm sure he'll be very tasteful,' said Jill thoughtfully.

'Won't you feel a bit murderous when you come to kill him?' I asked innocently.

'No,' said John. 'I've got used to the idea that he's temporary,' and he scratched Idi affectionately behind the ear.

John Rockliff had also been working on a welcome innovation at the southern end of the enclosure, a pit latrine.

The piglets that Idi should have fathered, brought onto the site the following winter. Brian with the trough, Peter Ainsworth and Helen looking on.

'There isn't a tree you can go behind in this area without getting an unpleasant surprise,' someone had remarked darkly a few days before, so some of the men had got to work on the pit. They boarded over the top with split ash logs and carved a circular hole in this floor, building up a strong cylinder of woven hazel with a neatly dowelled slat of barked ash logs on the top. The finished result of their labours was a neat, efficient and only slightly draughty latrine, with a modest wall of hurdles around it, later topped off with a conical roof.

Cleanliness was never a high priority with most people in the village, but they knew that the Celts had invented soap, and so John Rossetti tried to re-invent it with dreadful mixtures of ashes and pork fat. Meanwhile, most of the girls were concerned to find a substitute for shampoo. Sharon experimented with nettles quite early on, boiling them into a slightly slimy soup and washing her hair in that. But the result was not too encouraging. So they tried the clay method instead.

Lindsay cleaning Robin's teeth with a hazel twig.

The unit filmed Jill one day, washing her hair at the well. She had a tub of warm water and a gob of clay in her hand. As the camera followed her movements she plastered the reddish muck all over her hair and proceeded to rub it well in. Before long she looked like the victim of a Red Indian scalp hunter.

'It works quite well really,' she explained through the smears of clay, 'but you have to be careful to wash out all the bits afterwards. It really leaves your hair feeling, well, like hair again, once you've got all the clay out.'

It was noticeable that standards of cleanliness slipped more and more as time went by. To start with they all cleaned their teeth every morning using a chewed hazel twig with a frayed end, but after a while most people abandoned cleaning their teeth and only bothered to pick them with a sliver of bone or hardwood. 'You really have to work at it though,' mumbled Pete Little, as he probed away with a wooden pick, 'especially if you've been eating meat.'

Most people did not seem to be bothered by the dirt, but Lindsay objected to the wooden food bowls being unclean. 'Sometimes the dishes are greasy, after people have been eating meat . . . everything has a thin film floating on it when you have a drink. I think I'm getting used to it now though. I just drink without looking at it.'

For most of them the adjustments they had to make were more to do with their relationships with each other than being clean or dirty. I talked to Jill and Pete Little about the lack of privacy. 'Well, the way we are at the moment we haven't got any privacy at all and so when we go to bed at night we can't even whisper . . .'

'What about making love?' I asked.

'You have to get up very early or go to bed very early,' said Jill, practically.

Pete looked thoughtful. 'People go for walks a lot more than they did when we weren't all living under the same roof. I don't know what it means exactly . . .' He laughed gently to himself . . . 'but they do.'

By mid-May, the woodland floor was an endless carpet of bluebells. Here and there, as pretty and surprising as a snowflake, a single bell of the purest white set off the great blue drift around it. In smaller clumps were rarer flowers. Early purple orchids, their little pyramids of mauve florets, exotic against the woodland litter of dead leaves and the commoner greens and blues around them. Overhead the leaves had at last broken out on the trees, first the hazel, deep green and crumpled to begin with, then the beech and lime trees, brilliantly yellow when the sun shone fitfully through them, and finally the ash and oak, which towered over the hazel coppice in the clearing round about the settlement. The young oak leaves were deep orange when they first unfolded, a marvellous break of colour in a wood landscape which had been brown and grey for too many weeks. The villagers made prosaic use of the new growth, picking baskets full of lime and beech leaves, which they ate with enthusiasm, either raw in rather eccentric looking salads, or cooked like cabbage in a pot. They also nibbled at the little pea-like tubers of the pig nut, a feathery umbellifer which grew among the bluebells, and gathered large quantities of the bulbs and leaves of ransoms, a prolific member of the onion tribe, which sent up its broad fleshy leaves and starry white flowers on the grassy banks around the settlement. In fact the cuisine was beginning to improve. Everybody enjoyed garlic cheese spread, made by flavouring the lactic cheese with ransoms. Some of the more adventurous cooks started to invent their own recipes, like nettle and garlic soup, a blend of young nettles, ransom leaves and goat's milk. But they still had not really beaten the bread problem. And too little bread meant that everyone went hungry.

It was possible to bake a loaf or two at a time in a pit, as Martin had baked the Beltain cake. But with fifteen hungry mouths to feed, pit baking was not really practicable. Martin tried to build a clay oven in the half-finished house, but he made it too small, the walls were too thin and the rain never gave it a chance to dry out completely. After a few days it cracked and crumbled. The same problem affected the pots they tried to use for cooking. From the earliest days Martin had spent much of his spare time trying to make coil pots which would stand the heat of the fire. He knew that he had to add 'grog', an admixture of flint, or limestone, or even the ground up fragments of former pots, to the clay to enable it to withstand the thermal shock of firing. He also knew that it was theoretically possible to fire his pots, provided that the clay had been given time to dry out properly in a pit, or even in a bonfire. So he conscientiously wedged and grogged his clay before going through the time-consuming process of building up the pot walls, coil by coil, rubbing them smooth with his hands and a wooden spatula and putting them to dry in the least damp corner of the store house. Then he would build a bonfire in a shallow pit, and set the pots to fire in the embers, keeping up the heat by adding fresh fuel from time to time. But whenever he judged that firing was complete and started to rake through the ashes, he invariably discovered that half his precious pots had shattered in the heat. Most of the rest would be badly cracked and, if he did happen to fire a pot which looked flawless, it was only to provide a sick joke at his expense when the whole thing, full of aromatic stew, exploded on the cooking fire and scattered precious food along with its own fragments in the ashes.

The result was that one obtrusive piece of twentieth-century technology continued to rule the lives of the would-be Iron Age villagers. Dominating the fireplace, the very hub and focal point of the whole settlement, was a very large and much smoke-blackened aluminium saucepan. It sat there, a constant reminder of their failure to rid themselves of every vestige of the outside world.

But the village itself was taking shape. By the end of May all the outbuildings were finished and there was only a small hole remaining in the roof of the great round house. In the fields the green shoots of wheat, barley and oats were thrusting up several inches above the chalky soil. Almost all the livestock were in good health and so, too, were the inhabitants themselves. And, best of all, the sun finally burst through the clouds and transformed the whole settlement from a depressing collection of mud huts into a place full of life and hope for the coming of summer.

Chapter Seven

At the beginning of June there was a short spell of hot weather which raised everybody's spirits. Cow parsley burst into bloom in long white-topped waves on either side of the more open lanes around the forest. Hawthorn flowered and then elder, higher billows of white against the green of the trees. The woods were at their most beautiful, the orange bunches of new oak leaves freshly scalloped round the edges, the green of the lime leaves fresh and translucent. In the clearing, clumps of couch grass, dandelion and ragwort began to colonise the bare soil around the stockade. The villagers took off their heavy wool cloaks and robes and sat around in their underwear, the girls in their shifts, the men in improvised loin cloths, soaking up the sun.

The round house was finished at last. For the last few weeks of thatching, the hole in the middle of the roof closed more and more gradually as the workers scaled the straw slopes with more and more difficulty. In the end they decided that they could make a stronger and neater job by manufacturing a cone of hazel and straw on the ground and then hauling it up to the apex to form a pinnacle to the house. Kate and John Rossetti worked hard on this prefabricated rooftop to make it as robust and perfect as a cone of straw can be; then, one morning, with the film unit gathered below and the camera rolling, five of the men hauled their cumbersome burden slowly up the side of the house to mount it on the top.

They looked, as they ascended to the summit, like a parody of that famous photograph of the U.S. Marines hoisting the stars and stripes on Iwo Jima. Then John Rockliff nearly got his head trapped under the cone while making final adjustments and spoiled the effect. Down below, Helen and Sharon hauled on a rope to prevent the whole thing sliding to disaster down the opposite slope.

'Why do we always get the slave labour jobs while the men get all the glamour?' grumbled Sharon.

'Trust the men,' said Jill sourly. 'Whenever there's something to be done for the camera they're always out there, showing off.'

At last the cone was in place and the round house assumed its final, soon to be familiar shape of a giant, steep-sided, coolie's hat.

'All right it's all over! We can all go home now!' shouted Martin from the summit.

It was a moment for quiet, collective self-congratulation. The most difficult part, the toiling in the mud and the rain, was over.

The village in summer with the round house and palisade completed.

The villagers divided the inside of the house into thirteen partitions, previously marked out by the position of the pillars of oak which supported the roof. They all drew straws to decide on who got which space, the least popular positions being those closest to the doors. Luckily, the number of alcoves between the oak posts allowed space for a store house or a doorway between each sleeping cubicle, an arrangement that allowed for some small measure of privacy. Once allocated, each cubicle was then made more private by the erection of little interior walls of wattle, which partitioned off each bedroom from the rest of the house.

The evidence from excavations of Iron Age houses shows that very similar hazel partitions were built into many of them. In fact the arrangements may be far more ancient than the Iron Age because the site of Skara Brae in the Orkneys reveals stone-built so-called 'wheel houses' with almost identical internal alcoves, and Skara Brae is Neolithic, two thousand years earlier than this reconstruction. At the

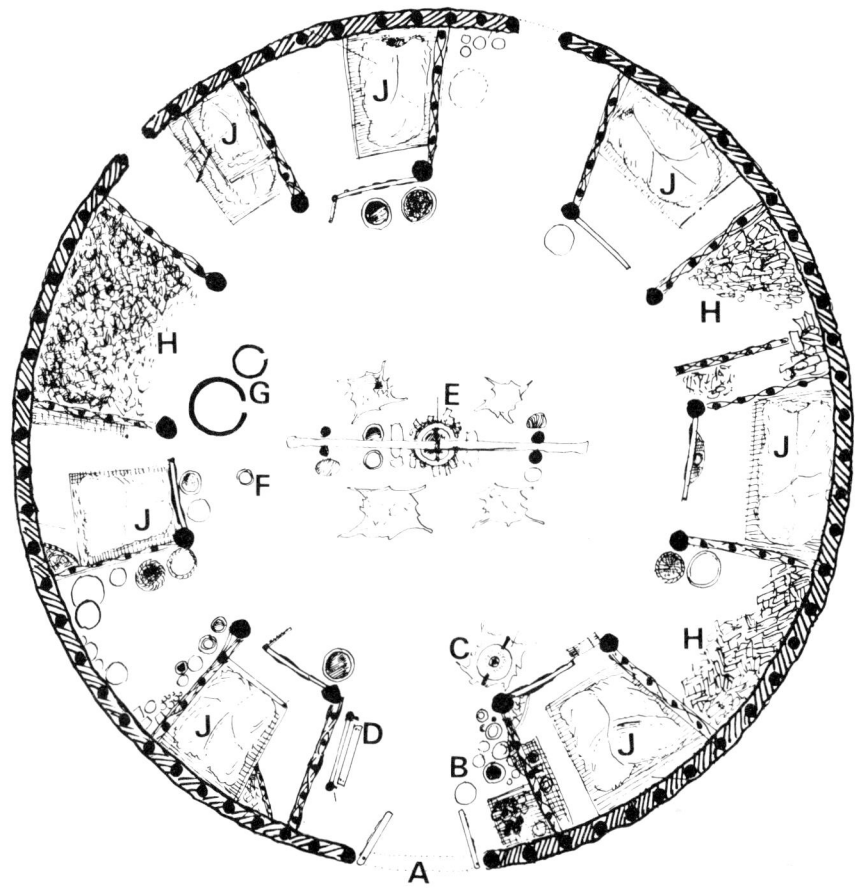

Plan of the round house as completed, later in the year.

- **A** Front door
- **B** 'Kitchen area', for storing food and utensils
- **C** Quern
- **D** Loom
- **E** Hearth, with gantry for supporting cauldron and skin mats
- **F** Blacksmith's forge
- **G** Bread ovens
- **H** Storage bay
- **J** Sleeping compartments

same time it is obvious that the villagers had needs which were almost certainly different from those of their ancient ancestors. They were still relative strangers to one another, whereas Iron Age villagers would very probably have been close relatives, all members of the same extended family and, apart perhaps from the wives, all knowing each other from earliest infancy. But no one really knows how the round house would have been used in prehistoric times. What was certain was that many of the people in our settlement needed privacy.

For some weeks tension had been growing between Lindsay and Sharon, with others being involved from time to time. There were many different minor irritations, inevitable when a group of people are thrown close together, but trouble centred on the fact that Lindsay was a vegetarian. Early on in the project she had resolved to try and eat meat, but she had found it impossible. Her husband Pete was also vegetarian, not on conscientious grounds, but simply because he disliked the taste. The couple had of course passed on their tastes and convictions to the children and though the boys did not themselves

Preparing food in the round house. Pots for setting cream cheese are in the foreground.

object to eating meat, Lindsay went to some lengths to try and provide them with an alternative diet.

There were several difficulties over this. In the first place the evidence from Iron Age sites demonstrates that the Ancient Britons ate meat whenever they could get hold of it. Animal bones, frequently with fractures showing where the marrow has been extracted, are one of the commonest finds in Iron Age refuse pits, so there was a problem over the integrity of the project. Then there was the difficulty of cooking separate meals. Although the Ainsworths co-operated as far as possible by accepting their vegetables cooked in meat stock, most of the cooks made some effort to keep the vegetarian meals apart from the rest. With constantly collapsing cooking pots this placed some strain on culinary inventiveness. Finally there was the problem of the foodstuff available. Meat was fairly abundant; so were dried peas, beans and stored hazel nuts and, in the spring and summer, fresh green vegetables. But many of the great vegetarian standbys like carrots and fresh fruit were simply not available though, of course, there was plenty of grain, which could be cooked in a number of different ways, even when bread itself was in short supply. Eggs were also scarce. The chickens were mostly Old English Game hens which produced a small flush of eggs in spring and then persistently refused to lay. When they did, these eggs were often lost to rats or other vermin before the Ainsworth boys could find them. Worst of all there was a great shortage of dairy products. The little flock of goats only produced enough fresh milk for drinking and a small surplus for making lactic cheese. When two of the Dexter cows calved, later in June, the milk supply increased slightly, but there was still very little available for hard cheese and the cooks found great trouble in making it satisfactorily without a plentiful supply of rennet and sterile containers. So cheese – hard cheese that is – was one of the rarest and most precious foods on the project. The Ainsworths' vegetarian scruples were not so extreme as to exclude eggs or cheese, and if meat was on the menu the cooks of the day had once or twice given the family special meals including one or the other. More often they did not and Pete and Lindsay would end up with a mess of peas and beans and precious little else. Lindsay herself may not have minded going without, but she had strong objections to depriving her children of the kind of food that she thought suitable for them. Unfortunately Sharon had also been a vegetarian, but had decided that the integrity of the whole exercise demanded that she eat meat, just like everybody else.

The row between them exploded quite early one morning in the little store house where the cheese was kept. Everybody else was out working or sitting about in the big round house, but the cries of rage which issued from the little hut were clearly heard all over the compound.

When attempts were made, later on, to patch up the quarrel, Sharon claimed that she had gone into the store hut and found Lindsay taking a piece of cheese for Robin and another morsel for herself. Lindsay denied eating any herself but admitted giving a fragment of cheese to Robin. Sharon accused Lindsay of stealing. There was a row and harsh words were spoken on both sides. No one interfered and the two women eventually parted without actually inflicting any physical damage on one another, but the reverberations of the quarrel could still be felt throughout the village for many days afterwards. The tension was so great that I tried to get the whole group together to discuss the problem, but everybody was anxious to avoid further friction and the quarrel was smothered, for the time being.

For most people, life in the village continued to improve. Throughout June each couple worked on and off on the furniture and fittings of their sleeping cubicles – their bedrooms, as everybody called them – though it seemed a grand term with which to glorify a little cubby hole of wattle. Certainly the bed took up most of the interior of each cubicle. The basic pattern was always the same, a flat hurdle structure with supporting wooden struts and the main supports keyed into the partition walls, a straw mattress, usually made by lashing little bundles of thatching straw tightly together, and a couple of large sheepskin rugs, each made up of four separate skins all sewn together. Most couples sewed the rugs together as well, making large furry sleeping bags, woolly side inward, which kept them snug and warm on the coldest nights. Pete Little introduced a refinement to the straw mattress. He revived the ancient art of straw mat manufacture, twisting a long continuous rope of straw which he wound round and round in a gigantic spiral, holding the rope together with a short tube of bone and sewing each succeeding coil on to the one before with the aid of a large needle made of a hollow tine from a stag's antler. Pete Little was also one of the first of the men to become adept at making hurdles, first splitting the hazel wands with a billhook and then weaving them horizontally between vertical struts of sturdier hazel rods. Sooner or later all the men got the hang of it. In fact the whole settlement was in a sense nothing more than a conglomeration of great hazel baskets and hurdles of varying shapes and sizes. This led John

Peter Little working on a mat. The straw is held in a bone ring and he is chewing his bone 'needle'.

Rockliff to speculate about some of the Iron Age tools they were using. All of these had been made in advance by the blacksmith, Ted Hart, who had worked from scale drawings of original Iron Age examples in museum cases, and John had put most of them to practical use over the previous few weeks.

'The axe isn't very good,' he explained. 'It's badly balanced and I think I've only used it once or twice, to cut a mortise in a big log of wood.' He took up another axe-like tool, but this time with the blade set at right angles to the plane of the handle: 'The adzes on the other hand are excellent, really useful. I've had hardly any experience using an adze before and I'm amazed how good a tool it is. I can't think why they're not used more today.'

He also had a little collection of billhooks. These were very carefully copied from Iron Age models, which may have been worn or rusted away long before they were abandoned for the archaeologists to find, and I had been worried that they were too light to be really effective.

'Yes they are light,' agreed John. 'They're more like spar hooks, the ones thatchers use, than a modern hedging billhook, but that's what makes me think that the Iron Age people used hazel a great deal. You see,' he lifted a little hook in his hand, 'this tool is absolutely ideal for hazel. You can use it to cut the stems from the coppice – provided

John Rockliff testing the sickle for sharpness. On the right, Sarah
is hard at work cutting.

they're not too thick – you can split hazel with it and you can use it very lightly, to get a fine point or whatever you want. As soon as you start using it you realise that it's tailor-made for the job.'

There were many other items in the Iron Age toolkit. Perhaps the most important of these were the blacksmiths' arsenal of equipment: tongs, hammers, small anvils, all very similar to those that are still in use in the twentieth century. There were small saws with the teeth set backwards so that they worked on the pull, rather than the push stroke. These survive in the orchard districts of England to this day in the form of pruning saws. There were also spoon-shaped augurs, similar to those illustrated in sixteenth-century woodcuts, small sickles for reaping and much larger crescent-shaped hooks for haymaking. And this was the main task that faced them now.

At the forest edge was a small, steep-sided meadow of about three acres. The grass was just beginning to flower, but it was not very tall and lush. No farmer boosted it with chemicals and the forest deer had

kept it grazed short until late in the spring, but this was the only grass available for haymaking. So every morning a small group of four or five villagers, armed with the long sickles, set off through the woods to the hay-meadow. It was very hard work. Traditional technique with a hook calls for the use of a crooked stick in one hand to hold the bunch of grass upright while the other hand brings the hook round in a sweeping cut. But the Iron Age sickles were thick and heavy to compensate for the softness of the iron, and they had very long handles. Examples of these have survived in the Somerset peat bogs and they suggest strongly that the heavier hooks were held in both hands.

The villagers bent to their task through the long, warm, June days. Pete Little had a splendid sweeping action, cutting great swathes ahead of the rest of the line of mowers, but even he complained of backache and all of them were exhausted by the work. They broke the day into two shifts, one group working until the cry of 'lunchtime' wafted faintly through the woods, and the other taking over for the afternoon and early evening. As the light began to fail they would gather up the hay that had dried out in the field over the previous day or two, stuff it into big baskets, and hump the baskets the half mile back to the compound. In this way they avoided much damage to the hay crop from rain. In a very wet year, with hay rotting by the hundred acre all around the county as it waited in vain for the baling machine, their hay was dry and sweet.

The labour was immense. Every wisp of hay had to be cut by hand, turned and dried with a wooden hay fork and then carried to the stacks which rose slowly in front of the round house. Their hands developed huge blisters, their backs and thighs ached from the stooping and carrying.

'It's the hardest work I've ever done in my life,' said Martin, as he sat, ashen and exhausted, at the end of a long day. 'Roll on the mowing machine.'

'Yes, or at least a scythe,' put in John Rossetti.

But scythes, like drains and main roads, had to wait for a few hundred years yet.

They made the hay ricks small and round, set on a foundation of brushwood to keep the lowest sheaves from spoiling, and piled around a stake, which gave some stability to the whole stack and provided a central pivot for a thatched roof. In the end six hay ricks of varying sizes occupied the space between the palisade and the round house on the north-eastern side. For the price of a bull calf they eventually had to buy in an additional three tons of hay, making about six tons in all, which Pete Ainsworth reckoned would see the livestock through the winter. In the event his estimate proved almost exactly right.

Haymaking left the group little time to do anything else, but the animals also had to be attended to. The first task was shearing the sheep. They did this out in the field, building a small hurdle enclosure at one end and driving the sheep inside so that they could catch each

Jill, shearing one of the Shetlands in June. John Rossetti and Peter Little are holding the animal down.

animal without too much difficulty. The Soay sheep shed their small brown fleeces without much help from anybody, but the Shetlands had far more intractable wool which had to be sheared laboriously by hand. John Rossetti held the sheep still, while Kate and John Rockliff snipped away at the fleece. Sooner or later almost everyone had a go, but it was not easy. There was only one pair of iron shears and it is a moot point whether these were permissible Iron Age equipment. Shears do occur on pre-Roman sites but archaeologists believe they were a rather late Celtic innovation, probably introduced in the second or first century B.C. After a while, however, the villagers stopped using the shears for other reasons.

'They're very slow,' explained Kate, as she tugged away at a prostrate sheep, 'and they tend to chew at the fleece. We find the best way is simply to pull the top layer of wool free by pulling at it gently with our fingers, but around the flanks it doesn't come off at all well, so now we use a sharp flake of flint and this works a lot quicker than shears. In fact we now think those shears are for cutting hair, because they're quite good for that.'

At sheep shearing time the cows also obliged by giving birth to a couple of calves. Betsy, the big Welsh Black cross, produced a hefty bull calf which she was determined to protect at any cost. The villagers had other ideas, because they wanted the milk for themselves and were determined to sell off the calf, using me as intermediary, so that they could import essential supplies into the village. But as soon as they tried to separate mother and son, Betsy went berserk. She went for Pete Ainsworth with her horns down and if she had caught him she would have killed him. He saved his life by leaping over the palisade fence, leaving Betsy in sole command of the compound. It took every available person and several hours of coaxing to calm her down, get her tied up in the milking shed and the calf into a separate pen. Even then their troubles were not over because Betsy refused to be milked, sent the pail flying with one well-aimed kick and knocked Pete out of the shed with another. It was several days before she was her normal calm, bovine self again.

The other beasts needing attention were the bees. These had arrived on the site rather late in the year and were housed in draughty hives made of wattle and coated with daub which was beginning to flake off in great patches. Pete Little, who had introduced himself to bee-keeping only the summer before, took it upon himself to look after the bees and the first task was to give them weatherproof homes. So without the benefit of a veil, or even a pair of gloves, he busied himself with the hives while the bees buzzed in and out, smearing new daub under the thatched cones which fitted over the hives.

'I don't use protective clothing because I don't suppose they had any in the Iron Age,' said Pete. 'What I do have, is a couple of leafy twigs here that I can hide my face in if the bees get really nasty.' Looking at the twigs and looking at the bees I decided that the advantage of Pete's leafy veil was purely psychological, but Pete did not seem to worry much about being stung.

'I make it a policy not to be alarmed by bees,' he said simply.

Brewing and baking were two other fields in which the villagers were beginning to make some progress. Pete Ainsworth was the brewer.

'I just soaked the barley overnight in a bucket and then put it in a basket to let it sprout. Then there was a bit of a business drying it out and trying to roast it and grind it. We managed after a fashion and then put it in half a barrel with some water and tried to get the temperature right using pot boilers – you know pieces of hot iron – and then left it to ferment. It's not too bad.'

The beer was flat and vinegary. Not too bad was perhaps over-stating the case, but at least the bread was now eatable. They had managed eventually to get a pit oven working efficiently, baking quite edible loaves in the embers of a fire in a hole in the ground, but the trouble was that it needed a very large pit and an enormous fire to hold more than one or two loaves and the pit method took a lot of time and trouble.

Martin finally succeeded in building a successful bread oven. This was a dome of clay with thick walls, built up layer by layer over a period of time, each fresh coat being left to dry before another was added. The first oven was only about two feet tall and two across. It was shaped rather like a bell, with a flat surface on the top and a squat chimney offset to one side. In a later model they dispensed with these refinements and made the whole thing a good deal bigger, but the original oven worked well enough. Every day one couple had the job of cooking the meals and another couple would bake the bread. In the morning they would bring in an extra load of wood and light a fire inside the clay dome. When the baker reckoned it was hot enough he – it was usually a man who had this job – would rake out most of the ashes, leaving only a few hot embers glowing inside. While all this was going on the co-baker, usually the woman, would be kneading the dough and shaping it into loaves. When these were ready they were left to stand for a while – there was no baker's yeast, but there is always a little natural yeast in the flour – and the loaves were then placed inside the oven on large flat stones. The entrance was then blocked up using more stones to stop the draught. To begin with they used turfs for this but found that these burned away too quickly to do the job properly.

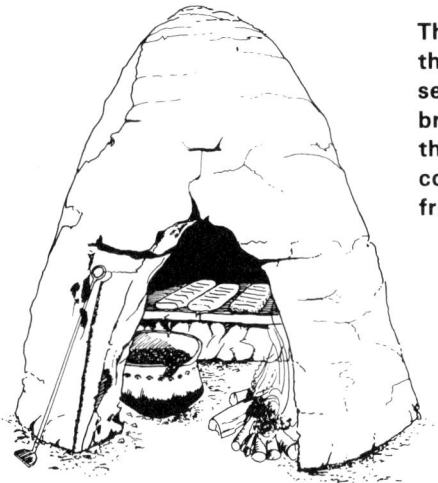

The bread oven. Normally the opening would be sealed for baking. The bread is on a stone shelf at the back and a stew is cooking in the pot in front.

The bread that emerged from this oven after an hour or two's baking was delicious. It was heavy, very solid in texture because of the lack of yeast and because the flour was rather coarse, but very good to eat. In a way it transformed their lives because they had a solid staple diet for the first time. The loaves were quite distinctive in shape, flat and rather elongated, but nicely rounded at both ends and with deep indentations in the crust to make them easy to break. Each loaf weighed between two and three pounds and during haymaking they were eating five or six of them every day. In summer time bread was eaten fresh at lunch time, usually with lactic cheese and a little butter if there was any. The main meal was then in the evening. Later in the year, when they could no longer see to wash the wooden bowls in the poor evening light, they changed the system and had the main meal at midday.

The querns – the flour mills – spun intermittently all day long. It was one of the most characteristic sounds in the village, a rather soothing, scraping, sawing sound as the stones turned. A quern is basically nothing more than one stone sitting on top of another. The grain is trickled down through a hole in the top so that it is trapped between the underside of the upper stone and the top of the one beneath and as the upper stone turns the trapped grain is crushed into flour. The stone on top has a concave base, the one underneath is convex, so the flour sifts downwards and can be gathered on a skin spread underneath the whole arrangement. Querning is slow, heavy work. Early in the year the couple responsible for baking the bread on a particular day also had to grind a day's supply of grain, but this placed an unduly heavy burden on the bakers. So a new procedure was worked out whereby everyone in the village had to grind two bowls full of wheat every day. The system was extremely efficient and the big flour jar was constantly topped up. The only snag was that the querns kept going wrong. The bottom quern stone had a wooden pin recessed into the top which engaged with a wooden pivot fitted into the central funnel of the upper stone. Constant grinding quickly wore away at this wooden bearing until the pin was too small and the hole in the pivot too large and uneven for a tight fit. The upper stone then wobbled alarmingly whenever it was turned.

Brian Ackroyd, Chief Quern Maintenance Man, spent many hours fashioning replacement pins and pivots, greasing the bearing to reduce the friction in an effort to ensure smooth running. 'The male bit's all right,' he told me, shaking his head as he delicately chiselled away at the bearings, 'it's the female part that's tricky.'

Inside the small round house. Peter Ainsworth is at work on the quern, baskets and a storage pot are behind him. Robin is dabbling in the salt barrel.

By the end of June tasks like these were becoming routine and the long days of haymaking were low on entertainment value. It was time for a break, and time to get away from the claustrophobic environment of the clearing in the forest, so a fishing expedition to a nearby lake seemed to be just the thing. It would give them all a bit of a holiday I thought, and also, with luck, provide them with some fresh fish.

The lake was long and narrow, tapering at one end to a reed-choked funnel of water which narrowed to an outlet leading to another lake below. This end of the lake looked to me to be ideal for a fish trap of the kind that Indians in the Mato Grosso seem to be able to knock up in a couple of hours. The idea was to build a solid screen of hurdles almost completely blocking the entrance to the narrow channel with an opening in the middle through which the fish would be driven. In a fit of enthusiasm I explained to the group how simple it would be. All they had to do, I assured them, was to walk the length of the lake in line abreast, beating on the water and generally stirring things up so that the fish would flee at their approach. The fish would then come up against the hurdle walls which extended out into the lake on either side of the narrow opening and the advancing line of beaters would force them through the gap and into the killing pool beyond. I had visions of great fat carp threshing in the shallow water while the villagers ran them through with improvised fish spears.

Duly impressed, the villagers agreed to try the scheme. They quickly built the hurdle trap and ten of them assembled at the far end of the lake, ready for the off. Naturally I had decided to film the whole episode and had borrowed a little flat-bottomed boat for the purpose. The intrepid camera team, David Saunders and Tom Brown, boarded this tiny craft and the even more intrepid producer prepared to act as a human outboard motor, propelling the boat through the water. It was a beautiful day. The dark, reed fringed lake was overhung all around with trees and the surface of the water plopped with the spreading rings of rising fish. A coot bobbed in the shallows and wild duck winged uneasily overhead. I felt exultant as I pushed the boat away from the bank and entered the shallow water. Then, horror! Black slime clung to my knees, then my thighs as I waded away from the bank with the little boat swaying in front of me. There was a vile smell of rotten vegetation. As the mud slopped and sucked at my lower limbs I began to get the first intimations that all might not be well with this fishing expedition. Then, as I waited, chilled to the marrow and up to my groin in mud for the approach of the beaters from the far end, I knew it was going to be a disaster.

The villagers had run into trouble before they even reached the water. From the bank it had all looked quite easy, but the approach at the end of the lake was obstructed by a tangle of stinging nettles and thorny brambles. When they finally got to the water's edge, already stung by the nettles and torn by the briars, they found that the water, let alone the mud, was far deeper than they had expected. Poor Lindsay, who cannot even swim, almost vanished from sight when she bravely slipped into the black depths.

From the camera crew's vantage point on the boat they at last saw a thin line of half-naked beaters advancing slowly towards them down the lake. David called instructions to me as he looked through his lens. 'Can we get over to that patch of reeds and frame the shot up nicely?' he said brightly, indicating a clump about forty yards of slime away.

'Yes, of course.' I laboured through the mud in pursuit of good pictures.

As the line of beaters approached it was obvious that they were too far apart. There were half a dozen gaps through which even the most stupid carp could easily escape, but the brave beaters kept coming, flailing the water and shouting abuse at the fish. I think it was the fish. As the water grew shallower I began to wonder how many full frontal mud-covered nudes the television audience could take, so I stopped the boat, which had been retreating before the approaching line of hopeful fishermen and allowed them to splash past. Then I swung the boat round behind them and the camera was rewarded with a line of bare bottoms instead.

The drive ended in the knee-deep shallows around the trap. Not one single fish was silly enough to swim ahead of the beaters and into the closed pool beyond. The villagers who had suffered so many painful indignities had the grace to laugh, but from that day forward they never took my advice again.

Chapter Eight

Fishing never really did provide the group with much in the way of fish, but it did eventually give them a good deal of pleasure. I had made arrangements with a local landlord to rent about half a mile of water on the river which flows along the valley bottom a few miles from the village. The river at this point is a delightful chalk stream, only about five yards wide, flowing fast and shallow over gravel through lush water meadows. It winds its way across a wide flat field where cattle graze to a place where the banks shelve steeply upwards and the meadow gives way to broad leaved woodland of oak and ash. In July the banks were thick with reeds, with the scented creamy meadowsweet and purple valerian, and the air hummed with dragon flies. The villagers gathered the meadowsweet because it contains salicylic acid, the main ingredient of aspirin – a more ancient remedy for headaches than pharmacists would have us believe – and dug the valerian root for use as a sedative. In the shallow water trout lay, noses to the current, holding their station in the water by imperceptible movements of fin and tail. The villagers may have admired their beauty, but they also lusted after them as food, so they came to the water laden with fishing tackle, long hazel poles, lines of linen twine and twisted horsehair. They also carried a bizarre collection of traps, roughly conical baskets of split hazel with funnel entrances at the broad end. These, when laid in the current and baited with offal, are supposed to tempt eels and exceptionally stupid trout. But the group never really mastered the mysteries of angling. They went fishing full of cheerful optimism, but not much confidence in their clumsy equipment.

On reaching the river they would first check the crayfish traps. These were just bundles of hazel rods tied together with a few scraps of offal. The crayfish wriggled in between the sticks to get at the decaying meat. When disturbed, instead of dropping back into the water they would cling on with lobster-like tenacity and ended up scrabbling in the grass on the bank. Unfortunately, most of them were very small and the group never succeeded in catching more than half a dozen scampi-sized crayfish at a time, which did not go far amongst fifteen people.

Fishing with a rod and line was a bit more effective. Bone fish hooks are a common find on Iron Age sites and the villagers manfully sawed away at tiny fragments of bone to come up with fair facsimiles. John Rossetti and John Rockliff caught three grayling between them one warm summer evening, enough to give everyone at least a taste of fish. But fishing took second place on trips to the river. On a bend in the stream, in the shade of a large alder tree was a deep pool of slower water tailing down to a shallow stretch bubbling over the gravel. On hot days Iron Age clothes lay in grubby heaps in amongst the nettles and meadowsweet on the bank and the river splashed with naked Ancient Britons. Fortunately, it was a quiet stretch of water, or earnest fishermen, intent on stalking through the reeds, would have been outraged to see plump white porpoises threshing about in the water and terrifying all the fish for a hundred yards in both directions.

These occasional forays to the river were one of the very few entertainments available in a life of hard labour on the farm. But even in the home settlement there were diversions.

In early July the village acquired a pair of baby polecat ferrets. These savage little animals are native to Britain and have been domesticated for many centuries, so they seemed a fair addition to the livestock and both the little polecats quickly became cherished pets.

Polecat ferrets.

Rush was a male, a little bolder and heavier than his sister, Wicker, and both were beautifully marked, with backs and chests of black merging into brown, and beige-coloured furry stomachs. Later on they were to become formidable hunters, but for the moment they were still learning their trade, darting round the compound, poking their noses into everything. They seemed to love being handled, disappearing happily up one Iron Age sleeve and popping out of another. They lived on eggs and milk and such scraps of meat as came their way, but even as babies they terrorised the chickens, sending them squawking and scuttering in a flurry of indignant feathers. Since the chickens were all inveterate thieves, adept at stealing food half-way between bowl and mouth, nobody minded very much.

The chickens also lived in terror of the other pet on the project, Blacky the crow. I had found Blacky, a miserable little half-feathered nestling, cowering in my orchard at home, with a distraught mother crow cawing at him from a nearby tree, and a marmalade cat eyeing him with unfriendly interest. I took him down the village and gave him to young Pete Ainsworth as a pet, but Pete soon tired of him and Kate Rossetti took over. She fed him on bread and milk, watched over him to see that he came to no harm and, when he was fully fledged, released him to fly at will around the compound. He would come to Kate's call and perch on her shoulder, take food from her hand and off her plate if he got half a chance. In fact he, too, became a thief, a pecker of the hand that fed him, and the bane of the chickens' lives. One day he stole a chick from Henrietta, a motherly little Bantam hen, and flew off with it to the pigsty with the chicken piping away for its life, as well it might. Hotly pursued by Sarah waving a stick, Blacky perched, still clutching the chick, on the roof of the pigsty. Sarah poked him smartly with her stick and he squawked into the air, dropping the luckless chick into the pig pen almost on the sleeping nose of Idi, the boar. Idi opened one eye, thinking it was tea time at last, gaped his tusky jaws and that was the end of the chick's short life. Perhaps it was just as well that Blacky's forays off the site gradually grew longer and longer until he eventually disappeared altogether, no doubt to plague the chicken runs and bird tables of the outside world.

The chickens, with the exception of Henrietta, and one or two other barnyard bantams which were included with our job lot of hens, were still not laying any eggs. Old English Game birds, bred for fighting and for show, tend to lay a fairly large clutch in the spring and then go on strike for the rest of the year. But would Iron Age chickens have been any better? The archaeological evidence is scanty. A few bones

The henhouse raised on
stilts to keep out foxes.
Underneath is a broody cage.

from a number of different sites suggest that the birds were smaller than modern varieties, and would probably not have improved very much on the Jungle Fowl of India and the Far East, the ancestors of our domestic breeds, which are no better as egg machines than the Game birds. Even the more prolific old varieties, like the Silver Dorking, come nowhere near modern breeds in egg-laying capacity. So the chances are that genuine Iron Age chickens would not have behaved very differently from the wretched Old English Game.

But the chickens did raise a problem of animal husbandry which applied in one way or another to all the livestock on the farm. As Martin pointed out: 'The chickens shouldn't be penned up. The sheep should be running out on the downs with one of us for a shepherd, instead of being fenced in all the time. The pigs should be foraging out in the woods, like the goats. So a lot of jobs we have to do with the animals, like taking them water in buckets and mucking them out every day, aren't really Iron Age jobs at all.'

This may have been true of summer, but in winter sheep would almost certainly have been folded on to home pastures and would then have had to be fed and watered – just as they are today. Pigs can also be herded, and were in medieval times, especially in the autumn when the nuts and acorns were on the ground. Goats would probably also have been taken out to browse on rough pasture, with a child or two in attendance, but goats can never be taken too far away from home in temperate climates, as they easily get chilled and drop dead with amazing speed. On the other hand the indications are that pressure on land was almost as intense in Iron Age times as it is today. With larger flocks and many competing neighbouring settlements, prehistoric farmers may well have had to keep their flocks confined by one means or another. Cattle raiding was, in any case, a favourite Celtic sport.

The unploughed chalk downhill still bears many traces of boundary ditches and fenced enclosures. With this in mind it was interesting to see the effect of the bank, ditch and palisade of the home settlement. It was authentic in its dimensions, but it was obviously totally in-adequate as a defence against marauding tribes. A small boy could easily jump the ditch and be over the fence in seconds. But although the defences were useless against human raiders, they certainly worked against animals.

'I've been thinking,' said John Rockliff, who devoted quite a lot of grave thought to the problems of Iron Age living, 'the ditch is on the outside, so it's obviously not designed to keep anything inside the settlement, or it would be the other way round. So it must be to keep the animals from coming in here and pinching all the hay, pulling the thatch off the roofs and messing up the houses.'

Once observed, it seemed obvious. The goats had already launched an assault on the thatched roof of their own house, nibbling a messy fringe all the way round the inside. To prevent this the villagers erected a barrier of hazel branches around the junction of roof and walls, but if the goats had been allowed to get at the outside as well, they would soon have made themselves a very wet and draughty home. The goats were in fact let out every day to browse in the woods, but the gate had to be shut firmly against them or they would be inside the compound, stealing everything they could get their teeth into. And when, later on in the year, the pigs were also let out and allowed to run free for an alarming few weeks, they too tried to get back inside and created havoc if they were allowed to do so. Only the ditch and bank with its flimsy hazel fence prevented them. The insight of experience like this may never convince archaeologists, but it certainly convinced the villagers.

The geese, which waddled happily round the clearing, were also inclined to sneak in through the front gate if anybody left it unfastened. Later on they were to prove skilful at stripping grain off the stalk before anybody had a chance to thresh it, but in July it looked for a while as if none of them would live long enough to do any damage. First the four goslings and later the old goose and gander all developed what looked like uncommonly bad colds in the head. Mucus streamed from the two holes on the upper halves of their beaks. Their eyes were full of greenish matter and they began to shed the small feathers on top of their heads. They all looked utterly miserable, refusing to eat and waddling blindly about in the most disconsolate manner. One gosling was so ill that it seemed kinder to put it out of its misery, and it looked as though the others would soon have to go the same way. I sought advice, both from a vet and from a delightful and extremely knowledgeable lady poultry keeper. The advice they came up with was to wash the eyes and beaks with a weak solution of salt and water in which the herb eyebright had been steeped and then rub a little grease into the mucus membrane around the eyes and nostrils. So every day the geese were herded into a little pen where Jill, Sarah and Pete Little administered the prescribed treatment. In a very short time the geese began to recover.

The geese put up with all the handling and the administration of grease and eyebright with remarkably little protest. 'They don't really mind. They make a bit of a fuss,' observed Sarah, as she released a flapping gosling.

It tottered a few steps, shook itself to adjust its ruffled feathers, straightened its neck and then waddled back expectantly, almost as though it wanted another dose of treatment. 'I think it's helped us understand one another, handling them like this,' said Pete thoughtfully, as he gazed deep into the gosling's eyes.

Pete Little was always gentle with the animals he handled, and gentlest of all with the bees. It was not a good year for honey, because there were spells of cold wet weather throughout the summer and there was never a really good nectar flow, when sunshine and moisture combine to produce just the right conditions in the wild flowers and blossoms. So it may have been sheer hunger which induced the bees to swarm several times in mid-July. Taking a swarm is not always easy, even with modern equipment; with no veil, not even a pair of gloves, it is a task to daunt the most resolute masochist. In theory bees do not sting when they are swarming. A cloud of bees issues forth in pursuit of a queen and for half an hour or so they fly hither and thither in apparently aimless circles. Then the queen settles, usually on a post or the branch of a tree, and the whole swarm gathers around her forming a solid mass like some great glistening fruit. At this point they are supposed to be gorged with honey, having taken on a full tank before leaving the hive, and for several hours, sometimes for a day or more, the whole mass hangs together, more or less comatose, while bee scouts and outriders hurry about looking for a

Peter Little putting fresh daub on the beehives. A cone-shaped straw hackle is in the foreground.

new home. When a suitable home has been located the swarm takes to the air again, flying in dense formation this time, heading straight for the new hive. If they are satisfied with their new quarters the bees quickly start to build new combs, the queen starts to lay eggs and a new colony is under way. The bee keeper's task is to try and short circuit this reconnaissance and induce the bees to take up residence where he wants them, in a new hive of his own. The correct technique is to approach the swarm with due care and discretion, break off the branch on which it has clustered, taking care to keep the whole mass intact, and then convey it to a clean white cloth spread at the threshold of a clean spare hive. The bees are then supposed to walk obligingly up an inclined ramp from cloth to hive.

Pete had a spare hive at his disposal, but it was in rather poor condition. The basket work was holding together, but great flakes of daub had fallen off the outside, letting in the air and light, which meant, of course, that the first shower of rain would render the inside of the hive extremely damp, and bees loathe wet living conditions. But when the Iron Age bees chose to swarm there was no other hive available. They swarmed, moreover, right at the top of a tall, slender ash tree, only a few yards from the home clearing. To get them, Pete would have to scale the tree, shin along the slender bough from which the swarm was hanging, break it off and somehow convey the whole living mass back down to earth and into its new home. He did not have a nice clean white cloth, nor was the tatty old hive particularly inviting, but the delicate operation seemed to be worth a try.

So Pete climbed the tree. Jill came up close behind him with a large basket covered with a cloth. Carefully, step by step, he made the perilous journey out from the trunk until he could almost reach out and touch the swarm. A few patrolling bees hovered close to his head, buzzing menaces into his ears. The frail ash branches swayed alarmingly and the earth was sickeningly far below. But a few feet below him there was Jill, the basket invitingly open. With calm deliberation Pete edged closer to the great shimmering ball of bees. His hand closed around the branch a few inches above them and levered sharply downwards; the green bough bent, but did not break. There was an angry buzzing as several hundred indignant bees separated themselves from the mass and flew furiously around his head. He tried again and the branch snapped. He swayed alarmingly as the resistance ceased, but somehow managed to hang on to the main branch with one hand, and the swarm with the other. In a few seconds he had the bees in the basket, the cloth over the top and Jill and he returned triumphant, bearing the basket full of buzzing insects between them. In the late afternoon they tipped the basket gently over at the foot of the hive and induced the bees up a series of twigs and into their new home. Miraculously, neither of them had received a single sting.

But the bees did not approve of their draughty new premises. Within two days they were off again, settling once more in the topmost branches of an ash tree. This time I took Pete's place and went after them myself, but when I at last managed to break off the branch on which the swarm was hanging, half of them fell away. Some landed in the basket which Pete was holding beneath, but many landed on his head and shoulders. Some even fell all the way to the bottom of the tree where Jill was propping up a ladder. By the time we got down both of them were covered in bees, in their hair, in Pete's beard, down their necks and up Jill's skirt. But the bees suffered themselves to be picked out of tangles and shaken off clothes without a single assault on an Iron Age person. I collected seven stings, mostly on my head and neck. Jill and Pete had none.

'I think it's something to do with the smell,' said Pete, absent-mindedly. 'Of soap, I mean,' he added kindly.

Soap, as it happens, still resisted John Rossetti's attempts at production. Most of the old recipes call for mixtures of animal fat, lye and lime. Lye is made by straining water through wood ashes, usually in a barrel lined with straw. Lime is traditionally manufactured by burning chalk or limestone at a high temperature in a specially built kiln. So far they had not succeeded in heating the rocks sufficiently to produce lime and most of the attempts at lye produced a greyish slop of ashes and water, with none of the caustic properties that proper lye is supposed to have. Undaunted, John Rossetti spent many hours stirring malevolent-looking liquids over a low heat.

'I can get it sort of soapy,' he said thoughtfully. 'I mean, it will take dirt off. The only trouble is that I prefer the dirt to the awful greasy mess that the soap leaves afterwards.'

So John stayed dirty. In fact they were all dirty. The inside of the big round house was always filled with a thin haze of woodsmoke, which turned into a choking fog when the baking stove was fired in the early morning. Everybody was kippered by it. Skin, hair, clothes, everything, was deeply impregnated, so that they smelt, quite sweetly but distinctly of woodsmoke. Their hands were dyed red with the clay, their hands, feet, elbows and knees carried the dust of the floor and the dirt of the compound, and their clothes gradually picked up a variety of stains from grain coffee or berry juice or old dried blood.

As long as the weather stayed warm most people washed hands and faces on most days. The rest of their exposed skin was usually covered by a light coating of greyish dust, but once every six days was the ritual of the bath. Bath time came at six-day intervals because it had to be fitted in with the baking rota. The extra fuel needed for the baking oven was also used to heat pot-boilers – odd lumps of old iron– which were fired red hot and then dropped, hissing and bubbling, into a half tub full of water. With skill and experience it was possible to heat a tub of water to bath temperature and maintain the heat by popping in another red hot pot-boiler at the critical moment. Of course it was also advisable to avoid dropping red hot iron on top of whoever happened to be in the bath at the time. Almost invariably out of every couple the first person in was the woman and the man got the dirty water.

For many of them the public nudity involved in taking a bath in front of a small crowd of other people would have been impossible in any other situation, but in the round house nobody ever seemed to be self-conscious. There was something about group living that made sexual voyeurism not so much distasteful as irrelevant. There were too many eyes and too many inhibitions about. Even a glance

Bath night. Lindsay in the tub and Sarah cutting up meat for supper.

across a smoky fire would instantly have registered with everyone else, so the project was high on nudity and low on rampant sexuality.

Keeping bodies clean was difficult enough. Clothes were washed by re-heating the bath water and pounding the garments in the tub, usually with the aid of a heavy lump of timber. The sodden gear would then be spread over the hot dome of the oven to dry or on the palisade fence if the weather was good enough. Fence-dried clothes ran the risk of being knocked into the dirt by a passing goat. Small items, like socks, might even be pirated by Blacky the crow and dropped in the pigsty. But oven drying also carried penalties. There was hardly anyone on the project who did not have at least one garment with a large brown scorch mark.

In the face of all these difficulties it was not surprising that cleanliness ran fairly low in the scale of most people's priorities. Lindsay alone worried about the lack of hygiene, like the habit of rinsing out the wooden bowls used for eating, standing them on the earth floor so that dirt clung to the bottoms and stacking them, dirt and all. When she noticed things like this going on she had great difficulty in restraining herself from making some disparaging remark. The trouble was that Lindsay's remarks had a way of making other people's hackles rise.

Groans and whispers would be exchanged, especially among the other women. Occasionally, there would be outright hostility, a sharp exchange of remarks which left a feeling of flat dislike in the air. Of course such exchanges were not unique to Lindsay. Almost everybody had to put up with some kind of character assassination at one time or another. Conflict between personalities was an inescapable part of their life, because there was no way of avoiding each other in the claustrophobic confines of the round house.

In the early morning hours everyone tended to congregate in the small area between the fire and the main door to the house. This was where cooking was done, where the quern was located, where people came and went all day long. Every action, every word of every person was magnified by proximity. After dark, when they gathered in a circle around the fire, there was still no escape from one another. The tone and inflection of a voice reached every ear, even when several people were talking at once, even when it was no longer possible in the gloom to recognise one another by sight. Even in bed, each couple in their own creaking recess, with the mice nestling in the thatch and scuttling on the floor, even then tense ears were alert for an unwanted voice raised in anger or protest on the other side of the house. There were no private arguments. Every disagreement affected everybody, all the time. They had nobody else to whom they could gossip, no friends outside the home in whom they could confide, nobody to laugh and joke with, nobody to yell at but one another. So quite small difficulties assumed enormous significance.

Conflict might have been far worse if everybody had not been working so hard, but haymaking was still in full swing. By the end of the day most people were too exhausted to do more than sit quietly around on the logs by the main entrance to the round house until the last of the light was gone and then make their way to bed by the red flicker of the fire. On fine nights when the stars shone bright in an inky sky some people moved their sheepskins outside and had the whole universe for a roof. The night sounds were not loud, the whooping of a tawny owl, the cough of a sheep in the field, the stamping of a fallow buck in the woods. Only the distant murmur of a jet plane high overhead in the night sky served as a faint reminder that there was still a modern world beyond the palisade. The villagers, isolated in their time capsule, had to solve their own problems in their own way.

Chapter Nine

On the first of August the group celebrated Lugnasa. This time they decided to have a holiday that they would really enjoy. They spent two days preparing food, querning extra flour, baking bread, gathering the fresh young peas and beans so that they would have as little as possible to do on the two-day festival. They also traded for a plentiful supply of cider and beer, because their own beer was still weak and vinegary. They planned the day's events with some care. It was to be a day of fun and games and the schedule of events sounded like a cross between a school athletics meeting and a party for children below school age. They had a race around the field (men only, dress nil), a 'putting the rock' competition, a tug of war, Indian wrestling (separate classes for men and women), all welded together with a little proto-Celtic ceremonial.

It was a blessedly hot and sunny morning. The children were the first to get the idea of painting themselves, daubing their small bare bodies with red stripes of wet clay, but before long everybody was doing it. Martin insisted on having his hair plaited, which certainly added something to his air of good-natured savagery. Helen painted his face for him, but he wasn't satisfied. 'You're ruining my chances of becoming a sex symbol,' he complained.

Brian and Pete Little had drawn straws to play the good and bad spirits in a ritual confrontation between Good and Evil, to be enacted later in the day. Brian solemnly plastered himself all over with white clay and wood ashes to give himself an aura of goodness, and ended up looking like some bit part player from a horror film. Pete Little, daubed with animal fat and charcoal, looked like an amateur black face minstrel, except that his great mane of yellow hair escaped most of the charcoal and hung in ropy tangles around his shoulders. Most of the girls were less ambitious. Naked to the waist in the bright sunshine, they stuck flowers in their hair, clay on their faces and looked like the inhabitants of some coral island before the missionaries arrived to spoil the fun.

For once during that wet, inclement summer, a heat haze hung over the woodland fringes at the edge of the clearing. There was a steady hum of insects in the still air.

The party seemed to take a long time to get under way, but at last the whole group were gathered in the field and the games could begin. By this time, however, perhaps because they were mostly a little bit drunk, the lust for competition seemed to have left them. They sat around or lay on the grass, giggling weakly at each other's efforts to 'put the rock'. Each competitor in turn stood at the mark, took up a heavy lump of limestone and hurled it as far as he or she could manage. But no one seemed to care who won. Not before time, because the black grease on Pete's body was beginning to be streaked with runnels of sweat, they eventually decided that the moment had come for ritual battle.

Pete strode out into the field in the space between his audience and a great pile of timber intended for the evening bonfire and waved a large wooden club while he boasted of the prowess of evil. But just as he was beginning to run out of lines, Brian jumped out from behind the bonfire, white and ghastly with wood ash and the power of Goodness. He was also armed with a club and for a while they capered about, from time to time remembering to shout threats at each other. The battle was brief: a feint with the club from Brian, a long lunge from Pete, then victory, a smashing blow over the head from Brian which shattered his club and laid Pete prostrate on the turf. Fortunately, Brian had spent a long time searching for a suitably rotten branch of wood with which to lay low the powers of evil. The sheep, which had retired to the furthest corner of the field, looked on in quiet alarm while Brian crowed in triumph and the rest of the group rolled in the grass and applauded happily.

The line-up for the tug of war lay directly over the pond. Mixed teams of men and women took hold of each end of the rope, dug their bare heels into the mud and hauled. The teams were quite evenly matched, and Goodness Brian, who headed one team, at one stage looked as though he faced defeat and a ducking. Adroitly he managed to let his team be pulled around the edge of the pond and then, with a united effort, they hauled their rivals into the water. Poor Pete Little, still streaked with black slime, now emerged dripping with water and mud from the pond. Mercifully the sun soon dried the losers.

The last spasms of competitiveness were absorbed by Indian wrestling over a tree stump table top set in the log rectangle in front of the big round house. Celtic festivities, at least in the Irish myths, seem always to have included wrestling of some kind or another, but arm wrestling over a table was the only kind that the group could manage. So, two by two, they locked hands and set their elbows on top of the log and strove mightily with one another. Despite a good deal of cheerful cheating there was not much doubt about the winners. Pete Ainsworth triumphed over the other men and Lindsay proved the strongest of the women. Holiday goodwill and sweet temper softened defeat for everyone else.

The other mellowing influence, apart from beer and cider, was the prospect of a feast. All day the carcass of a young ram had been spluttering on a spit over a fire of glowing charcoal and the cooks had also prepared the rarest of treats, dried and smoked fish. Because of their lack of success at the river, fish was an unusual item on the menu and one of the few food commodities that had to be imported into the village. So a box of smoked mackerel, traded against the dwindling credit reserves from the sale of young stock earlier in the year, was an eagerly-awaited treat. Unfortunately, modern smoked fish is neither smoked nor properly salted. Outside a refrigerator it goes off within a couple of days. The mackerel, saved for a week specially for the feast, were decidedly overripe, the blowflies had got at it and the whole box was wriggling with maggots. When I realised what had happened I was horrified. It seemed such a pity that they should be deprived of a treat, not because it was a delicacy unobtainable in an Iron Age context – the most primitive peoples all over the world have mastered the techniques of preserving fish – but because modern technology has produced a food that is pleasantly mild and moist, but offers no resistance whatsoever to the forces of decay. But I had underestimated the resilience of the villagers once again. Cheerfully, if a little covertly, the cooks picked off the maggots, cut away the worst of the rot and piled the remaining fragments into a large wooden bowl. Almost everyone had second helpings.

That night, still slightly tiddly after a day of drinking, the group lit a big bonfire in the field and sat around on the grass, talking happily. The break had come at just the right time, at the end of the long labour of haymaking and before the harvest started coming in. They were proud of the great stacks of winter fodder they had brought in and they knew they could expect a good harvest. Their buildings were complete, their livestock had produced healthy progeny, and they were beginning to get on top of the technical problems that had plagued them in the early weeks of the project. But what really cheered them was the prospect of the long-anticipated summer holiday.

As the Producer I have been criticised for loading the villagers into Landrovers and carting them off to the seaside for a few days, just like any suburban family in the Western world, but I had a serious purpose in mind. Iron Age people are known to have traded salt all over Britain, indeed all over Europe. In Southern Britain one of the starting points for the salt trade was the coast of Dorset, especially the Isle of Purbeck region. In this area long flat ridges of blue lias, a soft sedimentary rock, run far out to sea from the crumbling cliffs of the shore line. In summer the tides leave shallow pools of salt water on the flat beds of rock, which are then evaporated by the sun, leaving a thin encrustation of salt on the rock surface. Where natural forces showed the way, early man was quick to exploit the opportunity. By Iron Age times there was a well-established salt industry on the Dorset coast, and the clay moulds used to encase the blocks of salt are found far inland from the sea, enabling archaeologists to form some idea of the extent of the trade. In all probability the salt industry, even then, was in the hands of specialists who had mastered the techniques and hung on to the franchise, as it were, like modern monopolists. But it seemed to me at least likely that it was a seasonal industry and that the specialists had to turn their hands to fishing and farming when the weather was against them. I wanted the villagers to try and work out the techniques for salt making and sea fishing, to see whether they could also become self-sufficient in these essential skills.

In the event it did not turn out like that. On a rather showery day in early August I took Kate and John, Martin, Helen, Sharon and Brian down to the Dorset coast. They bumped along in the Landrover, making cheerful comments on the passing modern scene, excited and stimulated by very ordinary things.

'Did you smell fish and chips then?'

'Look at those colours, aren't they incredibly bright?'

'My God isn't it noisy?'

But they were still insulated by movement, cocooned in the vehicle. The world itself was a television programme flashing before their variety-starved eyes. There was no way they could reach out and touch it, but the experience made them buoyant and a little rebellious. Away from the village they were no longer serious minded Iron Age villagers, just a bunch of would-be holiday-makers.

The stretch of coastline I had chosen was on a remote country estate which certainly should have been far from the madding crowd. The rocky shore was not flat beds of lias but tumbled masses of limestone, with a great, uneven shelf of boulders and luxuriant vegetation along the bottom of the steep, sloping cliffs. At intervals on the cliff face tiny runnels of water emerged from cracks in the rock and dribbled down to form little pools of brackish water, choked with sphagnum moss and surrounded by tall reeds. All along the undercliff tangles of bramble fought with hawthorn, gorse and elder to form a low jungle of thorns hiding deep, leg-breaking crevasses and holes in the ground. On the beach itself the tide raced and swirled between the piled boulders, but here and there were little beaches of shingle where a bare-footed bather could pick a cautious route to more open water, and beyond the beach, stretching away to the west was a magnificent vista of cliffs glaring ivory white in the distance where lias and lime-stone merged into the near vertical crags of chalk.

The showery weather gave way to brilliant sunshine as the little group of villagers toiled their way down the cliff to the beach. Each person was encumbered with a bizarre load of Iron Age impedimenta – here a small barrel full of water, there a hurdle to form an instant roof for a hut, but they also brought with them their rolls of sheepskin bedding, a great funnel-shaped basket fish trap, a couple of rather alarmed chickens and, tagging along at the rear of the procession, Nina the goat. It was all too apparent that the apparatus for a three-day camping holiday has made some remarkable progress over the last two thousand years.

On the beach itself, just beneath the shelf of the undercliff, some adventurers had already erected a little shack of boulders and drift-wood. The villagers decided to build their own hut close beside it and use the shack as a refuge for the goat, but Nina, delighted by the goats' paradise all around her, promptly took to the jungle of the undercliff and all day long her white back bobbed amongst the shrubs as she ate her way to perfect goat content.

Using the hurdles they had brought with them they quickly con-structed a hut with a steep gabled roof and low walls of piled up rocks. To thatch it they cut reeds on the undercliff and carried back great bundles which they laid along the hurdles, making little effort to tie them securely into place. In fact they seemed rather unenthusiastic about the whole business of hut building.

'We came here to have a bit of a holiday,' grumbled Martin, 'not to build a rotten old hut.'

'Anyway,' agreed Kate cheerfully, 'we can always sleep out. The weather's fine enough.'

And for the moment it was. Brilliant sunshine brightened the cliffs and glittered on the sea. With the hut half complete, all six of them peeled off their clothes and bathed naked in the shining water.

That night it rained. The makeshift shelter with its poor covering of flimsy thatch was totally inadequate. The water came through the roof in steady trickles which were far harder to bear than the driving rain itself. So, with the waves pounding on the shore and the rain drumming on the roof, they all huddled together with the goat in the tiny fisherman's shack, which was more weatherproof, though far smaller, than the hut they had built for themselves. By all accounts it was a long and uncomfortable night and the new day when it dawned was still grey and miserable. Salt evaporation and sun bathing were both lost causes. Somehow, perhaps simply because they were in different surroundings, the Iron Age holidaymakers managed to keep their spirits up, but they all developed a fresh appreciation for the comforts of the round house.

'When that rain was bucketing down last night,' remarked Kate, as she tried to dry a wet skirt over a smoky fire, 'I thought of the round house and how dry and comfy it is and for the first time it seemed like home.'

The rain continued. The group who had gone to the coast changed places with those who had stayed at home, but the weather was so bad that after a day or so the second group had to be brought back to the site again. The whole seaside episode was literally a washout. Curiously, everybody seemed to have enjoyed it despite the wretched weather, but the excursion had an unsettling effect on all of them, making them more aware of the restrictions on their lives and less content to live from day to day within the confines of the site. They had been reminded that there was a world beyond the woods, and the temptation to explore it was stronger than before.

About a week later Martin went out one morning saying that he was going for a walk. Several hours later he had still not returned. Helen, growing worried, walked through the woods to the place where we had arranged for a telephone to be available in case of emergencies. She got through to me at home, saying that Martin had disappeared and that she had no idea where he had gone. I did my best to reassure her, but we both knew that there was little we could do but wait and see if he returned. Helen went to bed that night alone, in a great state of anxiety, because for some months their marriage had been going through a bad patch. I had assured her that he would come back and in fact I was almost sure he would, but the fact that no one had ever left the project gave the gesture an added significance.

When Martin himself telephoned early the following morning it was from a seaside town nearly thirty miles from the Iron Age village. He had gone off for a long walk, he said, to think things out. Now he wanted to go back. I was furious. I had arranged to spend that day with my wife and children, one of the very few occasions when we could be together during that long and difficult year.

'You'll just have to wait,' I told him. 'I'll pick you up this evening.'

I went to the village to tell Helen that Martin would be back soon, but it was not until after nightfall that I reached the place where Martin and I had arranged to meet – underneath the West Pier at Bournemouth.

The streets that evening were thronged. I found the pier ablaze with lights and packed with people enjoying themselves. Underneath on the beach, with the great iron structure looming overhead, I found Martin. He was wrapped up in his tartan cloak, his hair tangled and shoulder length, his rough woollen smock and trousers tied at the waist by a thong of leather with a large iron knife stuck through it. He looked like what he was, a refugee from another age, surrounded by the modern crowd in nylon shirts, jeans and flowered dresses. His feet were bare.

'Why haven't you got your shoes on?' I asked.

'I thought they looked a bit conspicuous,' he said. And grinned.

It turned out that Martin had walked all day and half the night, arriving in Bournemouth in the small hours, and had passed through the silent streets unnoticed. He had then spent the day on the beach, sitting on the sand with his shirt off and his trousers rolled up just like all the other holidaymakers. He had brought some bread with him, so he did not even eat any modern food until I brought him some fish and chips. He ate the fish, but refused the chips on the grounds that they weren't 'Iron Age'.

It was impossible to stay angry with Martin for long. Helen was furious when he came back to the village, but before long he had convinced her that the gesture was necessary. He had made a break, taken an initiative, done something that was not controlled by someone else, and now he could begin again to be a proper husband. To judge by the slow growth of confidence in Helen over the next few months, he succeeded.

The seaside holiday had been timed to coincide with the lull in the agricultural year between hay time and harvest. For a few weeks, from the moment the last of the hay was brought in and stacked to the time when the barley was ready for cutting, there was a chance to get on with a number of jobs which had to be set aside when everyone was busy in the fields.

Brian made use of the long August days to make more pots. The breaking pot problem was not quite so disastrous as it had been in the early weeks because the group had now been presented with a large bronze cauldron, copied from an Iron Age example in the British Museum. The cauldron was splendid, huge, heavy, and plenty large enough for the biggest stew, but the cooks still preferred to have additional cooking vessels at their disposal, so that they could have one pot for stew and another for hot herb tea, or one pot for meat and another for vegetables. So cooking pots were still much in demand. Unfortunately, the sturdiest pottery continued to crack and crumble in the fire.

One of the main problems seemed to be the clay. A large quantity of reddish clay from a commercial pit a few miles south of the project had been brought on to the site at the beginning of the year. Heavily grogged with crushed limestone this eventually produced durable cooking pots. But the fishing expeditions to the river had revealed another source of clay in the banks of the stream itself. Brian brought baskets full of this lumpy greyish stuff back to the site and began to fashion pots from it, wedging it carefully and extracting the worst of the weed roots and big stones, but leaving a great deal of the rubbish, small pieces of gravel and vegetable matter, still in the body of the clay. When the pots were dry he lit a fire in the bottom of a pit, waited until the embers were glowing and then stacked them in the ashes, slowly building up more fuel around and above them until he eventually had a blazing bonfire in the pit. After a few hours, when the embers had cooled sufficiently to be raked clear, he would extract a higgledy piggledy pile of pots, very few of which ever cracked in the heat. The river bed pots, grey and lumpy with bits and pieces of rubbish, proved more durable at the time than the smooth products of

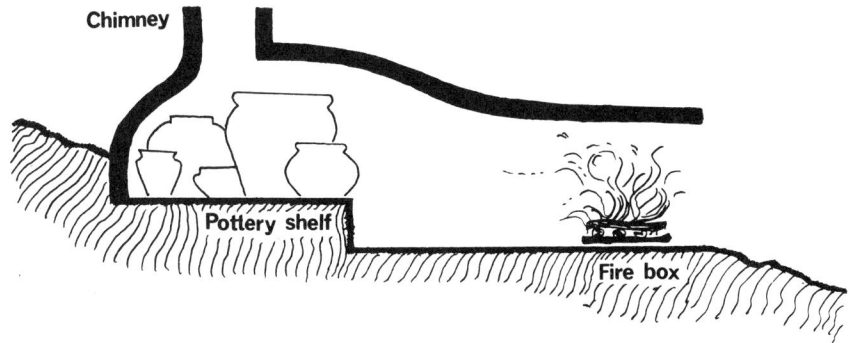

Brian stoking the kiln.

Martin finishing a pot.

red imported clay, which had to be grogged stiff with limestone before they would even survive the first firing.

But Martin was determined to devise a way of using the red clay more effectively. Using a framework of hazel branches he built a tunnel shaped kiln of clay with a firebox at one end and a low chimney at the other. Beneath the chimney was an earthen shelf on which the pots could be placed for firing. By building up a fire in the entrance slowly and carefully it was possible to control the firing temperature. At least this was the theory. In practice what happened was that Martin spent days weaving a complicated tunnel-shaped basket of hazel, days more coating it with layer after layer of clay, smoothing it off carefully inside and out and then, after all his labour, disaster struck. Perhaps the wicker framework was too weak to hold the structure together, or perhaps the clay superstructure had not been allowed to dry out properly. Whatever the cause, the kiln developed an alarming list to port and the first time Martin lit a fire inside it, nasty cracks appeared, running right through the fabric. 'Oh sod it,' said Martin and kicked the thing to pieces. Then slowly, painstakingly, he began to rebuild the whole complicated structure all over again.

Leather proved a rather more tractable material than clay. Sharon put her leather working skills to the test as soon as her shoes began to show serious signs of wear. Throughout the summer many people went barefoot most of the time, but thistles and sharp flints were everywhere and some kind of footwear was obviously going to be essential in the winter. So Sharon made a pair of sandals out of a piece of hide. Because the leather was thin she cut out two pieces for each sandal, using her own feet as a template. She then made a leather sandwich for the soles, packing grass padding in between the layers of leather. With an iron punch and a hammer she made neat little slots all around the rims of the soles, sewing them together with waxed linen thread and making a toe thong for each sandal. The finished articles looked a bit like something from an ethnic curio shop, but they worked well enough and as soon as Sharon was flip-flopping around in her own pair she was inundated with orders from everyone else wanting sandals of their own.

Jill was perhaps the most determined and competent craftswoman on the project and she was anxious to try her skill at weaving. Spinning was one of those jobs which people would do intermittently whenever they had nothing else on their hands, but weaving had to wait until the loom was ready. The men set it up just inside the front door of the round house and later in the year it was joined by another, made by

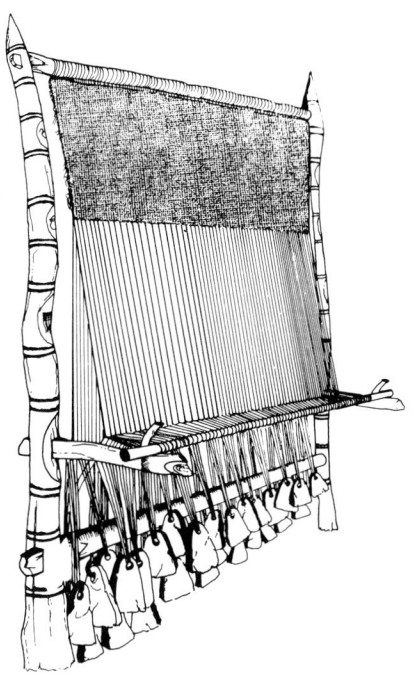

A warp-weighted loom.

John Rockliff, similarly positioned inside the back door, so that two people could weave at the same time no matter how bad the weather. Both were warp-weighted looms of a type known to have been used in Iron Age Britain. The structure consists of two uprights about seven feet tall, set into the ground at a slight angle away from the weaver. The uprights are joined at the top by a horizontal bar from which the warp, the vertical threads, are suspended. These threads are secured at the bottom to weights made of pottery or stone which give tension to the warp. In Iron Age examples these are of characteristic triangular shape, and loom weights, often still in the positions where they were abandoned when the last piece of cloth was completed, are some of the most easily identified finds on Iron Age sites.

About two-thirds of the way down the frame is the heddle bar, a horizontal rod to which alternate warp threads are attached. When the heddle bar is drawn towards the weaver and rested on a pair of pronged supports, a gap, or shed, opens up between the alternating warp threads. The weaver then passes a horizontal thread, or weft, through the shed from one side of the loom to the other. When the heddle bar is released the drag of the weights pulls a different array of warp threads backwards and opens up a new shed. The weft is then passed back through the new opening and the whole process begins all over again. In order to pack the weft tight and keep the cloth close-textured, the weaver has to use a flat piece of wood or weaving sword, which is inserted into the shed and used to slam the threads tightly together. The technique is laborious and time consuming, but slowly, thread by thread, the cloth creeps down the loom from top to bottom. Jill stuck doggedly to her loom, stopping every now and then to fiddle with a knot or adjust a warp weight, or hold earnest consultations with the other girls about what exactly was going wrong and why. Eventually a stretch of cloth, a bit wonky at either end and a bit pinched in the middle, began to take shape. In the weeks ahead all the girls were to take a turn at weaving, and the cloth they produced was warm, close-textured and surprisingly handsome to look at.

They dyed the wool from which the cloth was woven with a wide variety of herbs and flowers from the woods and fields round about. The most successful colour was the soft ochre derived from St John's wort, a delightful yellow flower which bloomed in a clearing in the woods. After various blotchy experiments they also got a warm golden orange from chips of yew wood, soaked for several days with skeins of wool. They also experimented with dog's mercury, nettles, blackberries, various lichens and tree barks, and got a range of rather muddy-looking shades. Most of the dyeing was done by Jill and Kate, though all the girls had a go at it and Martin got a splendid purple out of elderberry which faded to bluish-grey after a few weeks. They had not mastered the art of fixing the colours with a mordant, even though a supply of alum (a naturally occurring mineral salt) had been brought on to the project.

'You're supposed to be able to use human urine,' explained Jill cheerfully, 'only it's supposed to be stale urine. Well we've tried it stale and we've tried it fresh, but it doesn't seem to work. Perhaps our urine just isn't strong enough.'

Despite the lack of brilliant Celtic colours, the cloth had bands of rich brown and deep gold woven into it and it promised warmth and comfort for the coming winter.

Pete Ainsworth was also looking towards the future. Although the crops were still green in the fields he knew that autumn ploughing would have to follow hard upon the harvest if there was to be a realistic prospect of getting a fine tilth on the land for the spring sowing. He began to make a plough. Strictly speaking a plough is a machine for turning a furrow, folding over the top layer of soil with its mantle of grass and weeds so that it is buried under a wave of fresh earth. The instrument that Pete made is more accurately called an ard and it consists simply of a long beam, to be fixed to a yoke, and an angled piece of timber with a sharp point to gouge a deep scratch in the earth. The share on an Iron Age plough was no more than a pointed shoe of iron. The coulter, the broad blade behind the share, did not come to Britain until the Roman invasion.

The first of the autumn crops was the honey harvest. In August the last of the wild blossom came to an end once the lime trees in the woods had finished flowering, and it was time to get the honey out of the hives before the bees ate it first. Until quite recently, when the modern type of hive was invented, the beekeeper was faced with one of two choices, either to kill the bees by smoking them out, or to try and separate the bees from their honey. Pete Little and John Rockliff resolved to try a method known as warping, driving the bees from one hive into another. The only trouble was that the bees did not want to be warped.

Armed with improvised veils made by wrapping linen cloth around their heads, they set to work on the one hive which looked likely to contain a fair quantity of honey. First they set up a ring of stakes of about the same diameter as the hive. Then they inverted the hive, still with the honey and most of the bees inside it, within the circle of stakes, and placed a second empty hive over the open base of the first. Following the instructions of a veteran beekeeper they then began to beat the walls of the full hive with the palms of their hands. In theory the bees were meant to crawl from the full hive into the empty one, but they refused obstinately to do so. John and Pete drummed away and a handful of bees reluctantly made the journey to their new home. The others just sat tight and prepared to be nasty.

In the end they just had to break out the honeycomb with their bare hands and take their chances on being stung. As usual, perhaps because of Pete's calm and gentleness, the damage was small. Twenty thousand insects with enough collective venom to kill him a dozen times over allowed him to rob them of their precious stores and get away with it. But the harvest was not impressive. By squeezing the combs in his hand over a large pottery jar Pete managed to extract about fourteen pounds of sweet smelling honey, enough to last the community about fourteen days.

'It's another disaster really,' admitted Pete ruefully, as he scraped the last sticky drops into the storage jar. 'Still, we got plenty of wax.'

Fortunately, the field crops were much better. Towards the end of August the villagers began to harvest the barley. The grain was ripe and the ears were full. The only difficulty was the weather, black clouds gusting across a grey sky with intermittent squalls of rain and the occasional flash of sunshine. In the drier intervals the whole group turned out in the fields and began to gather in the crop. Four or five of them chopped away with reaping hooks, taking the straw almost down to ground level, while the rest came behind, scooping the barley up in large bundles and trudging back to the round house with them. The weather was too unreliable to leave the crop out to dry.

Soon the inside of the round house seemed to be packed with barley straw, with piled up sheaves in every available storage space, but as with the hay it was remarkable how little of the crop was lost to bad weather. As soon as it began to rain they could simply stop harvesting, gather up the cut grain remaining in the field and get it under cover before the rain soaked it. The remainder of the crop still standing in the field took no harm from a wetting. If, instead of doing the job bit by bit, they had devised some system for mowing the whole field at a single swoop they would have been unable to get the crop in before it rotted in the rain. As it was they succeeded in harvesting every stalk of barley in the glimmerings of fine weather between the squalls. Not for the first time the very simplicity of their technology was proving a blessing as well as a burden.

Chapter Ten

By early September all the barley had been gathered in and stored in the round house. As soon as the weather allowed, the villagers made the foundations for a barley stack close to the back door. The storage of grain is one of the techniques which archaeologists believe they understand. On almost every Iron Age site, at least in Southern Britain, there are large storage pits cut into the earth, anything from three to ten feet deep, and enough carbonised grain has turned up in these pits to make it clear that many of them were used as underground grain silos.

Experiments carried out by Peter Reynolds at the Butser Ancient Farm have shown that grain stored in a pit with the top sealed with clay will keep right through the winter to the following spring. The pit works like a modern grain silo. The bacteria responsible for decay require oxygen and, provided that all air has been excluded, the stored barley or wheat stops rotting as soon as all the oxygen in the pit has been exhausted. Unfortunately, as soon as the pit is uncapped the frustrated bacteria burst into life and the whole store speedily rots into a hot, fermenting, heap.

Unless there was some mysterious system for preventing this delayed decomposition it seems likely that pits were only used for bulk storage. Once uncapped the contents must have been speedily dispersed and eaten, or perhaps treated to an additional parching or drying process which may have arrested decay. The villagers, needing a constant supply of grain in relatively small quantities all through the winter, did not feel they could chance losing the lot, so they had to find an alternative to pit storage. The most obvious technique, because it was the traditional method for centuries all over Europe, was to store the corn, still in the ear, in stacks. Throughout the autumn and winter it could then be taken out, sheaf by sheaf, and threshed as need arose. So they built stacks which could be dismantled piece by piece. First they made a foundation of dry branches to keep the bottom sheaves clear of the earth. Then they built up the stack around a central pole which gave the whole structure some stability. To top it off and keep out the rain they made a portable thatched roof in triangular sections like large flat slices of cake which could be lifted on and off so that corn could be taken from the stack at any time and the roof popped back on afterwards. Within limits the system worked quite well, and the first stack of barley, together with a thick layer of oats, was erected early in September. The only problem, as they were to discover later in the year, was rats.

But the biggest difficulty at harvest time was the eternal law which dictates that everything comes ripe at once. The barley had been the first grain crop ready for harvesting, speedily followed by the oats and, a week or two later, the wheat, but there were also the peas and beans to take into account. The peas formed a thick tangle of herbage covering about half an acre. As long as they were still growing strongly the plants stayed clear of the ground, and from early July onwards the villagers had been able to gather the fresh green pods as a welcome alternative to the bullet hard dried peas which had been in store since the previous year, but when the field peas stopped growing in September, the pods full and tight, the first violent rain storm suddenly flattened the entire crop. The overstretched pods burst at the seams and peas scattered the wet earth. The leaves and stems lay in sodden swathes, and the smell of fermentation hung over the field. There was no time to be lost before the entire crop rotted on the ground.

While the rain continued to drizzle down, the whole group turned out and built long racks of hazel rods in the middle of the pea field. Then, laboriously, they hauled up the wet pea haulm and draped it over the rails. When the weather cleared the leaves and stems quickly dried out in the sun, and they were able to cram the brittle pea straw into baskets and carry it back, still with some of the withered pods attached, to the round house. With piles of unstacked barley in one area and piles of pea straw in another, the round house was crammed with people and plants. For the first time the vast space, which had seemed needlessly large for so long, was cramped and confined. Storage was obviously going to be a problem. Meanwhile the field was littered with millions of sprouting peas, free food for the rooks and pigeons which flocked in to take advantage of the wasted harvest. The thought of all that protein going to feed the birds prompted the villagers to get the geese out into the field so that they too could grow fat for the winter, but the geese had an unfortunate habit of wandering into the standing wheat.

'What we need to do is to stake out the pigs,' announced John

Rockliff, who always had a scheme he wanted to try out and was never easily put off by any difficulty.

So, not for the first time, minds were applied to the problems of pig keeping. The marital difficulties of Idi had given rise to so much anxiety earlier in the year that the villagers had decided to sell him and get another boar in exchange. In due course they acquired another beast, if anything even larger and fatter than Idi, whom they christened, for some unfathomable reason, Percy. For weeks now Percy had been put through ritual encounters with the two females, Gudrun and Goldilocks, so far without result, but Percy did at least show some interest. It was only the young females, the gilts, which remained coy.

There was still just the faintest possibility that they would discover some inner wellspring of sexuality and begin to respond to Percy's advances, but it no longer seemed very likely. There was a shortage of fresh meat in the village and after some debate it was decided that Gudrun would have to make the supreme sacrifice. They would keep Goldilocks for a few more weeks to see if she and Percy could finally form a useful relationship. In fact, it later appeared that neither of these gilts was fully developed. They were both about twelve months old, well past the age at which a modern sow would have farrowed, but the wild boar blood and the restricted diet may well have delayed sexual maturity. As far as the villagers were concerned, however, this was academic. In return for some of the young livestock sent out of the village earlier in the year they had obtained four young weaner pigs, two infant boars and two little gilts. When these had arrived and been installed in the new sty, they decided to kill Gudrun.

It is one of the curiosities of the English legal system that although it is quite legitimate to kill a cow for domestic consumption by banging it on the head with a hammer, pigs must be killed by a method approved by the Ministry of Agriculture. In practice this means using either an electric shock apparatus to stun the pig before slaughter, or a pistol of the captive bolt kind. So although I knew that the villagers could manage the slaughter perfectly well by themselves I was obliged to get a local butcher to come down to the village with his so-called 'humane killer'. The humanity or otherwise of killing an animal is of course more a matter of how it is treated prior to slaughter than of how it is actually killed. With blithe unconcern the British public allows animals to be banged around in trucks, pushed around cattle markets in a state of terror and herded into abattoirs where the reek of blood sends them into a state of white-eyed hysteria. But let anyone

kill a pig in his own backyard with a butcher's knife and the law will call the killer to account. If such a slaughter were to be shown on television the whole animal-loving establishment would be in a state of outrage.

Gudrun came out of the pen willingly enough. Brian went in front of her scattering a few oats. The others made a little triangular enclosure of hurdles to prevent her running out and she snuffled her way happily across the yard. There was no suspicion in her movements, no trace of alarm. They brought her gently to the point where they had rigged up a heavy ash pole on a fulcrum of two shorter posts, so that one end could be raised with the aid of a counter weight. Then, while Gudrun still nosed around after the food on the ground, the butcher stepped forward and deftly shot her between the eyes. She slumped immediately. Two men caught a rope around her back legs where she lay, and then hauled her aloft. The first time the cord snapped, the heavy pole fell free and hit John Rossetti smartly on the head. For a moment it looked as though there were two corpses on the ground, but John shook his head and carried on as though nothing had happened.

John Rockliff was the appointed butcher. As Gudrun's carcass swung aloft the second time, he got two of the other men to hang on to her legs and buried his knife deeply into her throat. The blood ran freely and a bucket caught the blood before it hit the ground. The villagers rarely let anything go to waste if they could possibly help it.

As soon as the carcass was drained of blood they lowered it on to a bed of straw and set light to it, piling fresh straw on to the blaze and turning the pig this way and that to scorch off the bristles. As the flames died down, Martin and John Rockliff set to work with knives, scraping off the charred hair which remained.

'How do you feel about eating her,' I asked, 'when you've been looking after her for all this time?'

'Can't wait,' grunted John.

Lindsay and Pete Ainsworth watched the proceedings from a slight distance. Pete had helped at the time of the slaughter because he wanted to make sure that it was done cleanly, but since they were both vegetarians they could hardly share in the general enthusiasm.

Lindsay looked white and shaky. 'It just confirms for me that I'm right really,' she said, trying hard to speak in a controlled voice. 'I mean it's right for me, personally, to be a vegetarian.'

But Lindsay's children all joined in the spirit of the occasion, making cheerful remarks about the recently deceased Gudrun. 'Cor . . . isn't she fat?' said little Pete, as Martin ran a sharp knife through the skin of the pig's belly to get at the entrails. I had often watched the children petting and stroking her while she was rooting about in the sty.

'Doesn't it worry you at all,' I asked him, 'the thought of eating her?'

'Nooo . . .' Pete screwed up his face scornfully.

'But you used to be a vegetarian,' I persisted.

'Yeah, I know,' he laughed. 'But I still like meat. She doesn't give it to me, but I still like it.'

For the next few days meat was inescapable; meat was all around them. Martin and John Rossetti butchered the carcass into neat joints and packed them in a barrel with a generous layer of salt between each joint. They cut off most of the fat and the girls cut it up into little cubes which they placed in the cauldron and simmered gently over a low fire. In a few hours they had a large jar full of lard, and the remaining fragments of crisp skin were devoured eagerly by whoever could get their hands on them. The whole village was greedy for fat. The blood was kept in the bucket in which it had been caught and stirred continually until it had set into a blackish paste.

'If you don't keep stirring it turns into congealed lumps,' explained John Rossetti. 'So when it's set you stir in flour and wild garlic, ground up mustard seed and some marjoram and lots of salt,' he laughed. 'I put lots of salt in because I wanted it to keep for ages because there's so much of it here.' He indicated fat, black sausages and round black puddings hanging from the roof. 'We crammed some of it into the bladder,' he said, indicating a black ball as big as a melon. 'And some of it we stuffed into rags of old underwear which we don't use much anyway.'

Sure enough, the fat pillows of pudding revealed, on close examination, a stretched skin of blackened bloomers.

The head was made into brawn, but the last delicacy to be prepared, apart from the fresh pork which was eaten with enormous gusto, was an enormous string of sausages. Sarah explained the process. Cooking and preserving food was one of her specialities.

'Well, you take the intestines; this is the small intestine.' She held up a long ribbon of greyish gut which she had coiled up in a bucket of water. 'And you turn it inside out by forcing water through it. Then you scrape off the mucus membrane stuff, which is a bit messy, and then you can use it.'

Her husband John was busy pushing stuffing into one end of the gut, with rather dirty fingers. 'The stuffing's made of bits of meat trimmed off the carcass, and about half as much fat, and marjoram and a bit of flour, wild garlic and mustard seed.'

But the sausages were not a complete success. They hung from the rafters for several weeks, collecting smoke, to be taken down for one of the autumn festivals. The meat had shrunk and withered inside the skins and the stuffing was decidedly chewy. The black puddings on the other hand were delicious, moist and spicy, and they kept fresh for months. Eaten cold or fried in lard they provided a tasty addition to the diet, bloomers and all.

Once the drama of the pig killing was over the group went back to work on the harvest. There were nearly two acres of wheat to bring in and this of course was the most important crop of all. The barley and oats, already cut and stacked, was mainly for animal feed. So the wheat harvest was crucial. Once again, as they planned how to go about bringing in the grain, the vexed question of storage came up. In addition to the pits that are found on almost all Iron Age sites, there is a very common arrangement of post holes set in squares about four feet apart, which are usually interpreted as granaries. Working on this theory John Rossetti and John Rockliff built two square structures with platforms set on top of four posts about four feet above the ground. On top of the platforms they constructed woven baskets of hazel, topping them off with little conical roofs of thatch. The idea was to fill these granaries with ears of wheat, cutting them high on the stalk and leaving the straw standing in the field in the manner so often depicted in medieval manuscripts. Unfortunately, whereas medieval farmers possessed both threshing floors and flails with which to beat out the grain from the ear, neither flails nor smooth floors for threshing are found on Iron Age sites. This meant that they would have to devise an alternative method for extracting the grain. It seemed more sensible to start off with the ears on long straw rather than short, so that they could keep their options open on how they threshed the wheat and also make more use of the straw for thatching, basket making and animal bedding.

Accordingly they cut the wheat close to the ground, just as they had cut the barley and oats. But the stiffer wheat straw allowed them to stook the sheaves in the field before they brought them in. For a blessed few days the weather stayed fine. The reapers worked their way slowly and rhythmically across the field followed by another line of workers binding the cut wheat into sheaves and standing the sheaves to dry. From time to time they would change places in the reaping line, the women taking their turn with the men in the long, hard, back-breaking toil. Once the harvest was in full swing a third group of workers made great bundles of wheat sheaves, hoisted them on to their backs and carried them back to the round house until they had accumulated enough for another stack.

In one corner of the field, close to the forest edge, the deer had leaped the fence and nibbled away at the ripening ears. At first it did not seem that they had done too much damage, but as the line of harvesters worked across the field it became apparent that nearly a quarter of the wheat had been stripped from the stalks. This was especially infuriating because twentieth-century laws prevented the villagers from hunting, let alone trapping the deer. It seemed a bit hard to lose a quarter of their precious harvest without even the compensation of fresh venison, and the deer would have been very easy to catch. They left clear trails through the woodland which cried out for a deadfall or a snare and even the children knew how to go about making one. The deer were so bold that they would sometimes come out of the forest in broad daylight and the villagers would watch them calmly nibbling at the corn, but they could only scare them off, then shrug their shoulders and bring in the last of the harvest as best they might. In the end they abandoned reaping close to the forest and instead picked off the few remaining ears by hand, rubbing the grain out between their hands to make their daily bread.

With one of the last sheaves of wheat Jill made a corn dolly, a corkscrew of woven straw with a bunch of ears sticking out at one end like a shock of hair. I asked her what the dolly was for.

'I don't know really,' she said, 'but there are old stories that around the time that we are supposed to be living, rather more violent things happened at harvest time, that they used to kill somebody and put their blood on to the earth to ensure a good harvest next year.' She turned the dolly over and it stood on end, the shock of straw at the top like a tiny symbolic human head. 'I suppose this is just a substitute for a person,' she said, thoughtfully.

When the wheat harvest was over the only crop still standing apart from a few vegetables were the beans, which were still green and fat in their pods. Harvesting them would have to wait until the pods turned black and brittle in the autumn, but all around in the woods and meadows there was a second, wild harvest to be gathered in. Blackberries burgeoned on the woodland fringes, ripe, black and luscious, a compensation for all the tripping and tangling of the brambles through the rest of the year. The elder trees were also covered with bunches of the tiny currant-like berries. The villagers gathered them by the basketful and brought them back to the house to mix with honey and make elderberry wine, and before the trees were stripped bare by the birds they had gathered enough to make nearly thirty gallons of purple wine, rich, potent and warming on the winter days to come.

But one of the most plentiful supplies of wild food came from the meadows and parkland a mile or two from the settlement. Mushrooms of all kinds grew in the long grass and around the shade trees in the fields. Early in the morning one or two people would go out with baskets and come back laden with mounds of curious fungi. Some of these, shaped like a brown and glistening bun with a mass of spongy tubes underneath, were members of the *Boletus* family, delicious simmered in butter or thrown in with the stew. Others, like miniature umbrellas, were parasol mushrooms, the most tasty of all the fungi. Identifying these and avoiding the lethal death cap, which also grew in the woods, was one of the more demanding intellectual exercises. Fortunately, there were also plenty of more conventional mushrooms which the villagers ate until they were sick of the taste of them. A few, far too few, as it later turned out, were threaded on to strings and hung to dry along with the bacon joints and bunches of dried herbs on the smoky rafters.

The work in the fields and long expeditions in search of wild food aggravated the problem that had been testing Sharon's powers of invention the month before. Their footwear was wearing out. Throughout the summer there had been two schools of thought on shoes in the village, to wear or not to wear shoes. Pete Ainsworth, for instance, always wore leather moccasins with a second layer of hide wrapped round them. I asked him whether he had ever tried to do without shoes.

'I did once,' he said, 'for a day and a half.'

'Fancy that,' said Sarah, who was one of the barefoot brigade. 'For a whole day and a half his lily-white feet were exposed to the earth!'

'I worked a day and a half without shoes,' continued Pete, stolidly ignoring the interruption. 'I cut the ball of one foot with a flint and I got a big thorn in the heel of the other. I couldn't walk, so I put my shoes back on and they've stayed on.'

A little knot of villagers were sitting around in the sunshine on the poles at the front of the round house. They had just eaten, the sun was warm and nobody was in a hurry to get back to work. The subject, in any case, was near to their hearts.

'Some of us think that perhaps feet will get used to hard wear,' said Jill, staring at her dirty toes wriggling in the dust. 'In any case we aren't really able to go on making shoes at the rate we've been going through them, or at least . . . ' she corrected herself . . . 'the rate that some of us are going through them. Anyway, I still maintain that Iron Age people would have gone barefoot through the summer, just as people through the centuries have gone barefoot when they could, to save on shoe leather.'

The matter may have seemed trivial, but it was not. Walking barefoot involved picking a way over the thistles and nettles on the fringes of the field, treading delicately over sharp flints in the cultivated land. It involved stubbed toes, painful thorns, courage to brave the brambles in the wood. Those who wore no shoes did so out of the conviction that to live within the limits of an Iron Age technology demanded that they went barefoot. So an argument over shoes was to a great extent an argument about fundamental approaches to the project. The idealists always wanted to stick to what they felt were the rules of the game, however hard that might be. The pragmatists were always looking for a sensible solution to a problem, even if it involved compromising the spirit of the project. There was of course a large amount of middle ground, plenty of room for different interpretations of Iron Age evidence, and many people who felt strongly about some issues but not others. Nevertheless this division of approach underlay a great many arguments and was responsible for many of the tensions.

It would be a mistake, though, to imagine that differences of opinion made it difficult for the villagers to work together. As the year wore on, their solidarity and strength of purpose became more and more impressive. They seemed to be able to work as a team with very little discussion and no apparent organisation, even when their motives for a given course of action were quite different. Once the harvest was in, for instance, the group had decided by common consent that the next priority was to lay in a store of wood for the winter. There was already a large quantity of timber lying around on the edges of the clearing close to the settlement. Throughout the late summer John Rockliff and John Rossetti had gone out every morning and felled a few stands of hazel coppice for the goats to get at the leaves. The timber lay where it fell, and now groups of people went out and piled it into heaps and then carried the heavier poles into the compound where Pete Ainsworth swung an axe and chopped the long branches into useable lengths for the fire. A great heap of firewood, the size of a ten-ton truck, quickly rose in the centre of the enclosure. When everyone was working on one job like this, the only people not involved were the cooks and the bakers. These essential routine tasks were carried out by rota throughout the project. Occasionally one couple would swap with another because they had a particularly pressing job of their own that they wanted to get on with, but when there was an obvious priority, everybody worked together.

The fact that the whole group was close together in age was both a strength and a weakness. It was a strength in so far as everybody was fit and capable of work, a weakness in that it allowed for no automatic age seniority, no natural leadership based on the strength of skill and experience. The gap in age between Pete Ainsworth at thirty-two and Brian at twenty-nine was not big enough to be significant, especially as Brian never pontificated or asserted himself at all. The lack of children was probably more important. It did not bother me in terms of the credibility of the project, because the idea had never been to try to recreate an Iron Age community with all its beliefs and hierarchies, but the children did make a difference in the way people got on together and the way they perceived each other's problems. Lindsay and Pete had more to contend with than anybody else, and in the end it was the children that were to cause, through no fault of their own, the first and last break-up on the project.

Chapter Eleven

On a grey cool morning in early October, when the mist hung late over the round house, Pete Ainsworth and Pete Little put the cows to the yoke for the first time. The yoke was a hand-carved piece of ash with two semi-circular recesses cut to fit the heads of the two cows chosen for the job. In fact there was little choice because Mary was far too old and frail, Brigid was just about to calve, and the only animals fit to work were Betsy, a heavy-shouldered Welsh Black cross, and little Jacky, long-legged but small and lightly built. All through the summer all the cows had grown accustomed to being led to and from the pasture on ropes, and animals which had started the project wild and intractable were now quite gentle to handle. Nevertheless, fitting the yoke was to be quite a shock to them.

Pete Ainsworth had designed the yoke to fit over the heads of the cows. There are various systems for yoking cattle, ranging from the lightest of bars across the withers of the little oxen of South India and Ceylon, to the massive head yokes of Northern Spain and Italy. Most head yokes are fitted just behind the horns with heavy leather straps and pads across the forehead holding them in place, and the only yokes to survive from Iron Age Britain were evidently designed to fit the heads of the cattle, but whether they were mounted fore or aft of the horns is open to question. Pete Ainsworth preferred to place his yoke across the cows' foreheads with loops around the horns to keep it in position.

Together with Pete Little he kept the cows back in the milking shed and turned them so that their heads were close together, roping them to the posts in their stalls. Then they wrestled the cows' heads into the yoke, tying them fast with cord, and brought them plunging and fighting out into the compound. The poor beasts did not know which way to turn. Betsy put her head down, Jacky tried to throw her horns in the air and they lurched in cumbersome circles across the compound. All the time the two Petes stayed close to them, guiding and patting them, muttering commands and endearments to them all the while. Pete Little's animal language was always gentle, coaxing. Pete

Peter Little and Peter Ainsworth training the cows to the yoke.

Ainsworth favoured a more robust approach. Together they set up a strange incantation: 'Come on you bugger . . . good girl Jacky . . . Get up there . . . good girl, good girl . . .'.

The cows, white-eyed and fearful, alternately plunged forward or stood rooted to the spot, splaying their legs and refusing to budge.

'I don't think they like it very much,' observed Pete Little, with characteristic understatement.

Pete Ainsworth grunted agreement. 'Looks as though we'll have enough trouble getting them to walk in a straight line, let alone getting them to plough.'

But they were not really that easily discouraged. After a few minutes they coaxed the cows back to the stall, fed them a small reward of crushed oats and released them from the yoke. Every morning for the next three or four weeks they went through the same routine until the two cows were as close and as well co-ordinated as a pair of Siamese twins.

The grain harvest was now all stacked and ready for threshing, but the puzzle of how best to tackle the job remained. There is no evidence of threshing floors on British Iron Age sites, but all over the world where people still process wheat without modern machinery they have floors of wood or stone on which to beat out the grain. Systems for doing this vary widely. In the wheat growing districts of India, for instance, they yoke cattle to a rotating pole and drive them round in circles so that their hooves tread out the kernels from the ears. The Romans used to use a heavy wooden sledge which was also drawn round in circles over the sheaves of corn; in England, of course, the traditional method was hand flailing on a wooden floor, but these methods, or variants of them, would not do, because none of them was likely to have been used in Iron Age Britain.

But the villagers were both resourceful and ingenious. They set up a beam of split ash on twin posts about three feet above the ground. They spread hides underneath and then, holding a sheaf of wheat with one hand and a baton of wood in the other, beat out the grain over the beam. Eventually there were three of these threshing rails, one under cover in the small store house and two in the open compound. The interesting thing about these from the archaeologists' point of view is that the pairs of post holes dug into the chalk for each threshing beam closely match similar pairs of post holes found on many Iron Age sites. These have usually been interpreted as drying racks for hay or cereals, but the villagers ridiculed this suggestion as hopelessly impractical.

'We've got six tons of hay in those stacks,' Pete Ainsworth pointed out. 'Now imagine how many racks you would need for that lot . . . fifty? A hundred? Anyway, you don't need a pair of bloody great posts for a drying rack . . . and exactly the same goes for drying the grain. You'd need hundreds of racks for a decent harvest; anyway it dries in stooks in the field and keeps perfectly well in a stack.'

This was true enough, but one problem Iron Age farmers did not have to contend with was rats. The old English black rat, *Rattus Rattus*, did not arrive on these islands until sea trading with Mediterranean and Middle Eastern countries became extensive, probably in the twelfth or thirteenth century. It brought the Black Death with it when it came. The brown rat arrived much later. So Iron Age farmers could have stacked wheat with impunity, with nothing more damaging than mice, voles, and the birds of the air to contend with. But for the villagers, rats were a menace. They infested the stacks almost from the first moment they were built, eventually devouring well over a quarter of the stored grain and invading the house to steal any carelessly stored food supplies. At night they rattled through the thatch and scuttled across the floor, fighting, squeaking and eating whatever they could find. Sometimes they even came out in broad daylight, snatching food from the plates before it could be eaten, murdering unprotected chicks and stealing the few eggs which the hens managed to lay. Siri the lurcher caught a good few, pouncing as deftly as a cat and killing them like a terrier with a quick shake of the head. The polecats also earned their keep, disappearing like snakes into the stacks and down the holes which pocked the earth around the palisade, but even their efforts could not contend with the rats' formidable reproductive powers.

So the pressure was on to thresh the grain as fast as possible. This was easier said than done. The rail method was slow; threshing, in any case, was only part of the process. The grain which fell from the threshing bar to the skins spread on the ground beneath was still full of rubbish. Often complete ears would be knocked off with half the grain still inside them. These had to be sorted carefully out of the mass and placed in a mortar, an ingenious arrangement of split logs which Martin had embedded in the earth. With the aid of a long pestle the remaining grain was then pounded out of the ears, but even the relatively free grain was still inextricably mixed up with chaff. The whole mass, grain, chaff and all, was placed in a large flat basket and winnowed into the air, first by hand, then as they became more skilled, the whole basketful could be tossed in the breeze and the chaff would float free. But winnowing demanded the right weather conditions, and even with every individual threshing ten sheaves of wheat a day, with winnowing and pestling going full tilt, the stack dwindled only slowly, day by day.

Once threshed the grain could be stored much more securely in a rat proof wooden barrel or hung from the rafters in sacks, but even then it could not be used for baking without further processing. The querns, always subject to minor breakdowns, seized up entirely with the soft new wheat. The villagers had to devise a method of drying or parching the grain so that it would grind freely in the quern. The device for this was quite simple, but delicate to operate. They dug a shallow pit in the floor of the store house, close to the wall, and made a short passage through to a clay-lined vent outside. The pit was covered with large flat stones, slabs of blue lias brought back from the coast, surrounded by a box of split ash logs. A fire was then started in the pit and wheat spread evenly on the stone surface. As the slabs heated up the grain dried out, but there were snags to this, too. If the stones were too hot the grain got burnt.

'Sometimes the flour is like cocoa,' complained Sarah with a laugh, 'all black and gritty.'

'But the main trouble,' Sharon pointed out, 'is that you can't knead it properly. I suppose it destroys the gluten or something, because the flour won't stick together and the loaves won't rise at all.'

'I think our dirt intake has gone up somewhat since we started threshing our own grain,' observed Jill drily. 'Talk about wholemeal bread! Ours is whole chaff, whole sticks and whole stones.'

But the villagers accepted the gritty bread, as they accepted most things, with patience and good humour. Before long they had devised an alternative to the parcher, so simple and yet so effective that they could not imagine why they had not thought of it before. I came into the round house one morning and as my eyes grew accustomed to the usual smoky darkness I noticed a new rack placed on top of the beam from which the cauldron was suspended. On top of this rack was a shapeless bag, no doubt made out of surplus underwear.

'What's that?' I asked Sharon, who was sitting by the fire.

'Oh that's our new grain parcher,' she explained. 'We just stick the wheat in a bag and leave it over the fire and it dries out beautifully. No burning, no over parching, and it querns perfectly.'

So the parcher was abandoned and the querns spun freely, bearings permitting, for the remainder of the project.

The attention given to threshing and parching had distracted the villagers from full awareness of the fact that the entire harvest was not yet gathered in. Out in the fields the beans still stood, their pods now slowly turning black, but still with one or two green pods on each stem. Then one night there was a fierce autumnal storm, stripping leaves prematurely from the trees, tearing off branches as it howled through the woods. In the morning Pete Little went out into the field and was horrified to realise that most of the pods had burst. Beans carpeted the ground, already sodden, bursting their skins and all set to germinate within a matter of days. There was no possible way of picking up the beans that had fallen. The crows and pigeons were already doing that job far more efficiently, so the only thing to do was to turn everybody out and rescue what they could, stripping the sparse remaining pods from the stems and carrying them in baskets back to the round house.

'What percentage of the beans do you think you've lost?' I asked Pete Ainsworth.

'Oh ninety per cent,' said Pete gloomily. 'We're just salvaging what we can, but we've still got five or six baskets full, with perhaps thirty or forty pounds in each basket, say about two hundred pounds of beans all told.'

'So you could have had a ton or more?'

'Oh easily,' Pete assured me, 'but we won't even be able to eat this many before the end of the project, so it's not too much of a disaster.'

In the light of experience they decided that the half-acre or so of beans was far too much for a community of their size. Had they sown the seed more thinly over a smaller area they could have gathered them more selectively over a longer period of time, kept them clean of weeds and had a higher yield from each plant. But this, like so many other things, had to be learned by experience. In the event, the scatter of beans over the field gave them an opportunity for another experiment in animal husbandry. John Rockliff finally devised a harness for the young weaner pigs which were now growing fast. With the aid of this device he was able to drag the reluctant pigs over to the field and tether them to stakes so that they could carry out a salvage operation of their own, and he and Brian eventually rigged up a series of pig stakes which covered most of the bean field.

At first the complaints of the tethered pigs were loud and long. They would make tearaway runs to the length of their ropes, only to be brought up short in a tumble of squealing indignation, but at last they discovered the riches at their feet and nosed and rooted until there was not a bean to be seen, only a pitted stretch of newly-turned earth. 'It's a pity they're not a bit more thorough about it,' John Rockliff remarked, 'then we wouldn't have to bother with the plough.'

The chickens also took advantage of the harvest abundance, though they lacked the wit to travel the quarter of a mile to the field. For them the bounty was on the doorstep. They raided the stacks from the outside while the rats raided from within. Little Pete Ainsworth was now in charge of the chickens and this job suited him very well because his favourite pastime in life was watching the young cockerels and imitating their behaviour. As they preened and strutted, so did he. He would throw out his little chest in creditable imitation of a fighting cock, and crow as loud as they. With his cloak about him he would climb on a tree stump, cock-a-doodle two or three times, then flap his cloak wildly and leap from the stump. 'I sometimes think he believes he is a cock,' said Lindsay, resignedly. 'He's got a strong imagination, that child.'

When two of the chickens contracted some mysterious disease, little Pete described their symptoms in vision as well as sound. 'They've got droopy necks,' he said. His neck drooped and his head flopped grotesquely to one side. 'And they're choking, and shaking their heads.' He choked convincingly and his lolling head shook as he began to totter about in diminishing circles. 'And they make a noise like this,' an awful gurgling emanated from his throat.

Before young Pete added the art of dropping dead to his repertoire,

Martin put an end to the chickens' misery. Unperturbed, Pete conducted a personal post-mortem. 'When I looked in their faces . . . when I looked down the air pipes and in the beak, there was all mucus and stuff and they had all snotty stuff down their necks. It was horrible! Yuk!'

Fortunately, the disease, whatever it was, did not spread to the other poultry. Human sickness was also a rarity on the project, though one or two of the villagers had come down with a tummy bug which lasted for a day or two and then receded. Pete Ainsworth was hit by it. For three days he kept to his room, groaning from time to time and completely unable to eat. Martin was philosophical about illness such as this.

'Do you think we ought to do something?' I would ask anxiously, if one of them was confined to their beds.

'Oh they'll get over it,' was the usual cheerful reply.

Martin had a number of herbal preparations which he used to treat mild disorders. Willowbark and violets, a mild sedative and analgesic was one favourite. Martin gave himself violent palpitations by experimenting with deadly nightshade berries, which are a powerful heart stimulant, but he took care not to give untried remedies to anyone else.

The most serious medical problem without any doubt was the constant risk of injury and subsequent infection. With axes and adzes flying all day long it sometimes seemed to me to be only a matter of time before someone missed the log and took off a toe instead. All day and every day too, people were out working in the woods, sticking thorns into different parts of their anatomy, cutting themselves with splinters of flint or climbing trees and falling out of them. Miraculously, very few of the injuries seemed to be serious, but one day John Rossetti got a thorn into his finger. He thought little of it, but the thorn went deep and the small wound became infected and in a day or two his finger had swollen like a sausage. Still he seemed content to let nature take its course, but Martin was worried. He sterilised a bronze needle in the fire and lanced the ugly swelling. John bore the pain stoically, a quantity of pus and fluid drained from the wound, but the swelling did not go down.

After a week or so Martin called me over when I arrived on the site. 'I think John Rossetti should have antibiotics for that finger,' he said.

We had always agreed that we would keep modern medicines off the site unless they were absolutely vital and, during nearly eight months of Iron Age living, there had been no need of them, but we had also agreed that as soon as Martin decided that outside help was necessary it should be provided. I called in the local doctor, an extremely helpful and good-humoured man who took a benign view of the project. The antibiotics were duly prescribed and slowly, over many weeks, the swollen finger subsided to its normal size.

There were only two other medical problems during the whole year which demanded outside help, and both of them affected the children. One day Robin fell over and cut his chin. Martin ran to the caravan we used as a production base and took a dressing from the first aid box to draw the cut edges of the wound together. 'I didn't see why Robin should be scarred for life just for the sake of a few television programmes,' said Martin briskly. I entirely agreed, though I was always impressed by how far people would go to preserve the integrity of the project. But the other medical problem was far more tricky.

Nicholas, the Ainsworth's five-year-old, was always a bundle of extrovert energy, charging round the place and taking on the world with riotus confidence. One morning, during the summer, Jill found him stumbling about the compound close to the latrine, with his trousers round his knees, searching the ground with intense concentration.

'What are you doing Nick?'

'I'm looking for a stick to put my bottom back with,' he explained.

Mystified, Jill investigated.

Lindsay and Pete questioned Nick closely and discovered that he was suffering from a condition which Martin diagnosed as rectal prolapse, where the lower part of the gut extends through the anus. Whenever this happened little Nick would trot off, find a stick and shove it back again. He had not thought it worth telling anybody about it. The local doctor had been consulted over this too, but he did not think it necessary to take any drastic action, beyond discouraging the stick remedy, and Martin had, in any case, shown Lindsay and Pete safer and more hygenic methods of putting everything back in place. On the whole, the two doctors agreed that the food on the project was probably better for Nick's condition than a normal twentieth-century diet would be. The whole wheat and bran, which formed a large proportion of the Iron Age diet, gave plenty of roughage, good protection against all sorts of bowel disorders. It may have been some consolation to the villagers, as they chewed their way through their delicious, but undoubtedly gritty, bread, to realise how much good it was doing them.

The food continued to improve during the early autumn. Not only was there plenty of meat, peas, beans, and wild fruits and fungi from the woods, but the chickens had begun to lay again, once the summer moult was finished. There was also plenty of milk from the goats and cows, not enough to make butter unfortunately, but plenty to drink and to turn into soft lactic cheese. This was made simply by allowing the milk to sour until the solids curdled and then hanging the curds to drain in a muslin bag. There was always a bowl of milk set to sour close to the fire and a bag of curds hanging by the back door. Hard cheese of the conventional kind can only be made with rennet, which is extracted from the rumen, or milk stomach, of a very young calf. It is an enzyme which aids the calf in digestion. Old recipes for cheese include various methods of extracting the rennet. Some are blessedly simple, like filling the rumen full of milk and leaving it to set. Unfortunately, rennet will not keep for more than a few days without refrigeration, so Iron Age cheese making must have been finely geared to the maximum availability of milk and newly killed calves, both at the same time, a coincidence which is of course nicely timed by nature in the spring.

'We did try making hard cheese when we killed the last calf,' Sarah explained, in her best schoolbook manner, 'but it was too old, its stomach was full of hay – you know the rumen was fully developed and the reticulum –' Sarah was strong on biology – 'was tiny. We did what we could, but it didn't work properly.'

Despite the failures with cheese, their cooking was getting better all the time. Towards the end of October they made a number of what they called winter puddings with flour and lard, laced with honey and elderberry wine and stuffed with wild fruit, blackberries, elderberries and sloes. They were very good to eat and would probably have kept right through the winter if the group had been able to resist eating them.

The toil in the fields had ended with the bean harvest and now the villagers were able to settle down to the jobs which really interested them, the crafts which they had just begun to learn the previous year, but had been unable to practise since. These included weaving and the making of replacement clothes, tanning and leather work, basketry and of course pottery, which they had been obliged to try and master in the intervals between work in the fields.

Helen did a great deal of hard work that always tended to be overlooked, especially on the days the camera was about. One of her crafts was tanning leather and we came across her one day working on a lamb skin, which she had stretched on a wooden frame hanging on one side of the cow shed. Shyly, she described the process to me.

'As soon as it came off the animal we scraped the flesh and fat off the back of the skin. Then I stuck it in a half barrel in a solution of alum and salt and left it there for a few weeks and finally I stretched it on the frame by tying it on with cord.'

She demonstrated how to slip a pebble into a fold of skin, then fasten a cord around the little lump of skin with the stone inside it, and secure the other end of the cord to the frame. 'You must never make holes in a skin or it tears,' she warned. 'Then I scrape away some more to get the last of the muck off. This one I will just leave to dry out, but I'll keep working on it, scraping like this, and eventually it will dry sort of soft and crinkly, quite supple really.'

Helen scraped away conscientiously with an iron knife. 'Of course this isn't proper tanning,' she added, apologetically, 'just what's called alum tawing. I'll try tanning with oak bark later on, but it takes a long time and Kate wants this skin for a hat as soon as I can finish it.'

Jill was making another hat out of the skin of a rabbit which Siri the lurcher had caught. She sat in the main doorway, her back against the loom, sewing with a bone needle, her dark brows knitted in concentration. 'This is the third blasted needle,' she grumbled, as she stabbed at the furry bundle in her lap. 'It's made out of lamb's bone. The point continually needs sharpening because it wears away when you push it through the skin.' She paused, to rub the needle briskly on a piece of limestone. 'They're quite difficult to make really, because it's difficult to get a splinter of bone fine enough so it doesn't tear the skin and yet strong enough to get through stuff like this.'

Making clothes was now a major industry. Whenever the weather was too wet to work outside, a group of men and women would be gathered round the fire, all involved in different stages of clothing manufacture, spinning, sewing and knitting. John Rockliff seemed eternally to be spinning when he wasn't doing something else. His wife, Sarah, did a lot of knitting, as did all the other girls, except Sharon, who made a cheerful tangle of all the handicrafts she tried. Soon almost everyone had a jumper made with genuine Iron Age wool. Even Martin knitted himself a little wool beret which he wore at a rakish angle like some prehistoric onion salesman. Woollen leggings, socks, scarves were all produced at those fireside knitting parties. Knitting is a mysterious craft. No one seems to know quite when it was invented, and it is rare among pre-literate peoples even today, but it seemed to the villagers that so simple a technique must have an ancient pedigree, so whether Iron Age Britons knitted or not, the villagers did a great deal of it.

By the end of October there was a sharp chill in the air and in the early mornings and late afternoons the knitted scarves and sweaters began to come in useful. The nights now were cold and out in the woods the fallow bucks roared all night long, calling the hinds to their rutting grounds. The mist hung low over the clearing in the morning and the light was soft and golden when the sun eventually filtered through the trees, and now the leaves were just beginning to turn colour, the lime trees corn yellow, the beeches a rich brown and the birches a clear lemon colour, even lighter and brighter than the limes. Hazel nuts hung ripe on the trees, the best of them always high up above the ground.

John Rockliff went out with a billhook and chopped whole trees down to get at the nuts. 'Isn't that rather an uneconomic way of gathering them?' I asked. 'Not really,' said John, in his matter-of-fact way. 'We're going to need the wood anyway, and the goats appreciate the leaves.'

Sure enough the goats assembled magically at the sound of the billhook and began munching away at the leaves. They ate the nuts, too, shell and all, if they got half a chance. The goats had formed a herd with its own disciplines and hierarchies much more quickly and thoroughly than their human masters had done. Annabelle, an elegant black and white nanny, was the herd leader. As she wandered through the woods, browsing here and there, the other goats would follow, though at times her dominance would be challenged by another black and white goat, Easter, who was a far more obstinate and determined fighter if things came to that point. But most of the time Easter was content to let Annabelle take the lead and the other goats tagged along, each in order of seniority. Only Shaggy Maggy would have no part in goat hierarchies, but kept to her own path, usually hanging around the compound gates and waiting for a free handout and a bit of attention from passing villagers. The goats, like the human beings, had come to terms with their environment.

Chapter Twelve

During the second half of October a mysterious new structure appeared near the main entrance to the compound, just outside the garden gate. It was what seemed to be a huge tubular basket about eight feet long and two feet in diameter. I asked what it was, but people were evasive. 'Oh it's just something Martin's working on,' was the only response I could elicit from anyone. But I had my suspicions, and when the first tube was joined by another of the same size I knew for certain. Martin was making a giant.

One of the most famous Roman propaganda stories about their Barbarian enemies is Julius Caesar's description of how the Celts used to make a huge wicker cage in the shape of a man, fill the giant figure with captive enemies and then set fire to the effigy on a gigantic bonfire. The story may or may not be true. What does seem highly likely, in view of the human effigies found at the bottom of wells, in bogs and in other terminal places, is that the idea of making a model of a human being and then subjecting it to some awful fate was well established in Celtic Europe. The evidence from Denmark, to the north of the main Celtic sphere of influence, suggests strongly that human sacrifice was an established Iron Age practice. It is possible that the destruction of effigies was a refinement of this, a milder alternative to the sacrifice of a living human being.

The Celtic Festival of Samhain is conventionally assumed to have fallen on October thirty-first. By all accounts this was a fearful time, the onset of winter when the spirits of the dead had to be placated. The early Christians, with their shrewd capacity for turning pagan ceremonies to good account, whitewashed the whole thing and turned it eventually into All-Hallows Eve.

The villagers may not have been aware of this, but the urge to celebrate Samhain was very strong. By persistent enquiry they found out as much as they could about Celtic mythology and devised a masque, a ritual of their own to enact. The giant wicker man, a prehistoric Guy Fawkes, was the star of the show.

They made him out of hazel branches and the long tangled vines of wild clematis, old man's beard, which entwine the branches of many of the trees on the forest verges. When he was finished he was nearly twenty feet long, with an enormous barrel-shaped body, long tubular arms and legs and a faceless ball of a head. They dragged him to an area just to the east of the palisade, close to a little side gate in the bank, where a log bridge gave close access to the round house. Then, on Samhain eve, they began to raise him towards the sky. 'We all got a bit panicky when we realised how heavy he was,' said Sarah later. 'We thought we'd never get him up.'

They attached a rope to his neck and rigged up a couple of poles to act as an improvised crane. Then, with two men hauling on the rope and the rest of them heaving and lifting, they gradually raised him, continually propping him with stakes to give themselves a rest and prevent him from crashing back to earth. Martin was much in evidence, shouting instructions and pushing here, pulling there, until at last the wicker man stood erect. In his hand was a great spear, the trunk of a young birch tree, and around his feet rose a pile of branches, until his nether limbs merged with a great mound of timber. There he stood, huge and menacing, a fitting emblem of the powers of evil.

The weather was cool and damp. A heavy mist of fine rain enveloped the clearing and it did not look as though anything short of napalm would catch fire that evening. But the villagers had grown cunning in the ways of fire. John Rockliff supervised the building of the wicker man's funeral pyre and the giant himself was stuffed with straw. 'Don't worry,' said John, with his usual unflappable confidence, 'he'll burn.'

As darkness fell they prepared to enact their ritual. I later discovered that John Rossetti had been planning the scenario with some care. All the cast knew their parts and they had even devised costumes. Pete Little, as Levada, a manifestation of the Celtic sun god Lugus, stood radiant in a halo of wheat straw, which he had somehow fastened to his head like a two-dimensional Afro hairstyle. John Rockliff in a horned headdress, Jill and Kate with wooden masks hiding their faces, skulked in the bushes, harbingers of death and darkness. The good god Levada stood with a ring of villagers around him, handing out the harvest bounty: to one person a sheaf of barley, to another a basket of rosehips, to another hazel nuts and so on, so that everyone but the evil spirits received a gift of food of some kind. When this ritual was complete the group around the sun god began to chant his name in praise: 'Levada, Levada . . .'

Then the evil spirits arrived to spoil it all, attacking the god's defenders with vigorous blows from wooden swords and carrying off the hapless Pete Little into the darkness. There they covered him with a pile of damp leaves and crowed spookily over their success. But rescue was at hand. Brian, returning triumphant from the round house with a lighted torch in his hand – actually he had to go twice because it went out the first time – kindled more torches for the erstwhile defenders of the god, who now came to his rescue. Armed with light they drove off the powers of darkness. They carried Pete Little to the big bonfire, poured elderberry wine down his willing throat and then danced around the pyre crying 'burn him, burn him,' finally plunging their torches into the heart of the great heap of wood and straw.

Miraculously, considering the weather that night, the fire caught and soon the wicker man was impressively alight, flaming from his feet to his head. The sun god was alive again. The evil spirits also revived and came eagerly to the bonfire, hoping for a share of the elderberry wine which was now flowing freely. The masque was over.

Of course it was a travesty of a ritual. No one knows for certain what Celtic celebrations were like, and those which survived over the centuries, tamed by the Church and the passage of centuries, are probably distorted beyond the possibility of recognition by those who first devised them. But ritual is important to people. It gives them a sense of continuity, a kind of immortality, and if ritual is not there it is probably necessary to invent it.

The Samhain festival finished with a feast beside the bonfire. There was wine in abundance. Three of the young cockerels were roasted on a spit; there were slices of black pudding, hard-boiled eggs, great lumps of hoarded hard cheese, honey cakes and rather withered pork sausages, all eaten in the radiance of the great bonfire. Afterwards, when everyone was a bit drunk, they pulled out a half barrel full of water with crab apples bobbing in it. Everyone, including the entire film unit, had to have a go at snatching apples with their teeth, no hands allowed.

The last ritual for the night was the closing of the doors. The doors had been made with great labour over the previous two weeks. Pete Little had fashioned the frames, carefully tailoring selected boughs of hazel wood to fit the doorways at front and back. The girls had covered the frames with deerskin, carefully sewing them tight to make a windproof barrier. On the night of Samhain they closed them with some hilarity for the first symbolic time against the icy blasts and evil spirits of the coming winter.

The feast continued all next day with a lamb roasted over the embers of the bonfire and the wine still flowed down receptive throats. For the time being everybody was in high spirits.

Unfortunately, the goodwill was rather short-lived. For some time tension had been increasing over what others saw as Lindsay's uncooperative behaviour. The muttering and whispering had reached the point when Lindsay could not avoid knowing she was being talked about and this, of course, increased her sense of isolation. The others felt that she did not do her fair share of work, that she was prickly and stubborn. Lindsay, for her part, felt that she was being unfairly persecuted. Heavy, theatrical sighs could be heard if Lindsay aroused the least disapproval. As John Rossetti observed: 'It seems to be the women who feel the tension most – and create it. It makes me realise that being stranded on a desert island with a bunch of females might not be paradise, after all.'

One of the most persistent sources of friction was a continuing debate over what was or was not 'Iron Age'. There were quite a few breaches of Iron Age protocol, as it were, but there was a nice distinction between what was allowed and what was not. It was all right to drink modern beer or cider, because both would have been available to Iron Age Britons, whereas orange juice for instance would not have been. It was permissible to use an old plough share as a pot boiler, but not to hide a piece of old mirror glass. Compromises had been made over contraception, over letters home, over giving the children lessons, over the various medical matters; the project was viable only on its own terms and the rules had to be everybody's rules, or nobody's. For the rest of the group there was a broadly accepted consensus view, adjusted from time to time as circumstances changed and it was this group view that Lindsay could never entirely accept.

Despite the disagreements, most people still managed to enjoy life. One of the great recreations of autumn was rabbiting. A mile or so from the clearing in the woods the trees give way to open downland with glorious views over the bare, sheep-grazed hills to the distant purple haze of the south coast. A steep valley opens up at the foot of the highest ridge of the down, with high grass-covered spurs on either side. Here and there is a single hawthorn, bent and twisted by the winter gales, a few patches of gorse and, in the distance, a straggly wood of stunted ash trees, but pitted all over the turf of the down close at hand are hundreds of rabbit burrows, great interconnecting warrens which turn the bowl of grassland into some gigantic misshapen colander. Myxomatosis, the great rabbit scourge, has struck here again and again over the last twenty years, allowing the population to build up for a while and then laying waste the warrens once again. This year was not too bad. There were rabbits about, not too many, but enough to be worth hunting, and hunting was a recreation the group needed. Strictly speaking, rabbits should not have been the quarry because they are an introduced species, native to the Mediterranean, and were imported into England in medieval times as a table delicacy, probably by the Normans. Wild deer, both fallow and roe, were abundant, but deer hunting was denied to the villagers by law. The only other creatures which might have offered them a change of diet were the stupid hand-reared pheasants which wandered idiotically through their woods, and grey squirrels, introduced from the United States much more recently than the rabbits. In the circumstances it seemed only reasonable that rabbits should be fair game.

The villagers went after them in little groups of two or three, well wrapped up in cloaks and sheepskins against the wind and clutching two sacks, one empty and one with the polecats wriggling and squirming inside it. They would choose a warren, cover all the holes they could find with small slip nets of knotted linen thread and loose the polecats down a well-used burrow. After a while, just how long depended on the polecat's mood and sense of purpose, the rabbits would bolt, shooting like bullets out of their burrows to fly kicking and bucking into the nets. A swift blow on the head and the netted rabbit would be in the bag. Sometimes.

'We haven't got enough nets really,' explained Sarah, who was skilfully knotting cord to make another, 'so you have to miss some holes, and of course the rabbits always choose the holes you haven't netted. But we've been pretty successful. Helen and Martin caught five the other morning.'

It was amusing to see how these gentle girls, who would never have killed a mouse in normal circumstances, had become hunters. 'Yes it's good fun,' agreed Helen as she deftly slipped the skin off a dead rabbit, 'and rabbit stew makes a nice change from salt pork.'

Sarah and John Rockcliff were the owners of the only really skilled hunter on the project, Siri the lurcher. Siri was beautiful, built like a small deep-chested greyhound, sleek and black with milk white stomach, a dog that was always in evening dress. Emer, the other dog, was also a mongrel, but very different in build, large and shaggy with a deep bass bark and a slow, lumbering run. Emer was the watchdog, suspicious of strangers, always the first to give the alarm. Siri was absurdly affectionate, greeting everybody like a long-lost master or mistress, but she would nab any hare or rabbit that ventured into their little patch of woodland and bring it proudly home for supper.

By the middle of November Martin and Brian had finally mastered the art of making earthenware pots that would stand the heat of the fire. Martin's kiln had proved a great success in the end, and pot after pot emerged from the firing with a fine ring to it, and now at last they could be used for cooking.

'After seven months of experimenting,' Martin announced one day, 'we've actually managed to cook with them in the hottest part of the fire and they've come out absolutely unharmed with the bottoms glowing red hot, with boiling water inside, and that's about as much shock as any pot can stand.'

In fact, before the project ended, they were all making pots with such casual skill and confidence that they would simply stick them into the cooking fire in the round house to bake overnight.

The other great step forward was getting the forge to work. In a relatively unused area of the round house to the left of the front door, John Rockliff and John Rossetti scooped out a small hollow in the floor and lined it with clay. They made a small tuyère, a clay tube to conduct the draught from a pair of bellows into the heart of the fire. For fuel they needed charcoal which demanded a whole separate manufacturing process of its own. They dug a pit, lit a fire in the bottom and carefully stacked it full of weathered oak, chopped into chunks a foot or so in length, waited until the fire was going really strongly, then covered the pit with a thick layer of turf. After a day or two the fire burned out and the wood, black but not completely oxidised, was excellent charcoal. Armed with bellows, tuyère and charcoal, all they needed was a live ember from the fire and they were away. The bellows worked on a simple principle. It was no more than a skin bag with a tube at one end. Across the top were a pair of battens sewn into the leather which opened and closed the bag. Parted, the battens admitted air into the goatskin; closed, they shut off any other outlet for the air and the bag could be squeezed downwards, forcing the air out of the tube at the bottom. The tube was slotted into the tuyère and the tuyère into the little furnace. With a little practice the bag bellows could be closed and squeezed in one movement. In fact little Nick Ainsworth, who was fascinated by the whole process, quickly became the bellows worker, happily pumping away for hours on end.

The blast of air made such an efficient draught that the centre of

John Rockliff mending a pair of tongs.

the furnace glowed fiercely within a matter of minutes and a piece of iron pushed into the heart of the fire was soon red hot and malleable. Within half an hour of first getting the forge going the two blacksmiths were enthusiastically hammering and bending almost any piece of iron they could find.

The tools they had to work with were remarkably effective. Blacksmiths' tongs, almost identical to those which are still in use in country forges today, have turned up complete on Iron Age sites. Lump hammers and smaller hammers of varying shapes, small anvils, some of them even with the familiar modern beak have also survived intact. The two small anvils which John Rockliff had mounted in a tree stump were in fact modelled on a find from an excavation only three miles south of the project site.

From that day forward the steady rhythmic blast of the bellows and the metallic ring of the hammer on the anvil were two of the most characteristic sounds in the village; and the smoke from the forge, mingling with the smoke from the oven and the smoke from the fire produced at times an almost inpenetrable smog in the round house. The filth from the charcoal added another layer to the rind of dirt which tended to accumulate on John Rockliff's hands and face and his jerkin and trousers were stiff with dust. Industrial pollution is not a twentieth-century invention. But the two Johns were elated. They were mastering a new technology, the craft which once brought about a revolution, three thousand years ago, the revolution we now call the Iron Age.

Chapter Thirteen

The last of the yellow leaves fluttered from the trees around the clearing. The ground, like some richly tessellated pavement which has seen better days, alternated patches of green, scatters of dead yellow and gold with the bare brown earth. On frosty mornings the leaves scrunched underfoot, crisp as cornflakes, and the deep ruts and pot holes in the ground lay in wait to stub toes and twist ankles. Mist seemed constantly to hang over the bare trees, as though it somehow emanated from the forest itself, and over the great conical roof of the round house the smoke from the fires created the illusion of a vast bridal veil hanging from the mist above. On the rare bright days the sun sent shafts of orange light slanting through the trees, making long cathedral shadows over the clearing.

'The sun never rises above the trees now,' said Jill sadly, gazing at the shadows. 'You have to go out on to the down if you really want to see it.'

'I can't make up my mind which is worse,' said Pete Little cheerfully, 'the frost that freezes your feet off or the mud that bogs you down up to the ankles.'

'But we're never cold in the round house,' Sarah reassured me. 'In fact with the doors closed it's often too hot.'

'Yes, I've seen the odd hairy chest about in the evening,' observed Jill, looking sidelong at Martin.

'And we've all seen some people looking a bit off the shoulder round the fire,' responded Martin.

It was true that the round house was remarkably warm. In the daytime, even with both doors gaping to the cold air to let in what little light there was, the area round the fire was always warm. At night, with the doors closed it was, as Sarah had said, almost too hot for comfort. After the evening meal people would spread their sheepskins on the uneven floor and gather close around the fire, chatting, spinning, one of the girls might be knitting and one of the men whittling a knife handle or making a thumb pot from clay prepared earlier in the day. The fire would be banked up brightly, not for warmth but to provide extra light. So, as the evening lengthened the

132

circle widened as everyone withdrew from the heat, often to lie on the bare earth floor and gaze at the firelight flickering on the polished beams of the roof. Not that they were really polished, but the smoke had formed a shiny black carbon surface on the rafters and dyed the thatch a deep orange, the straw also seemingly varnished by the smoke until it shone. Thick black nets of cobweb, heavy with soot, spoiled the illusion of zealous cleanliness.

Archaeologists used once to believe that the fire hazard inside these round houses must have been a constant risk, and I had worried about it myself. But the sparks which swarmed towards the roof seemed always to die before they reached the black pocket of constant darkness, just beneath the roof cone itself.

On the nights that I stayed in the round house I would sometimes spread my sleeping bag close to the fire as it slowly burned down. The villagers had a system for keeping it burning all night. The cooks for the following day – in practice it was always the man who was responsible for the fire – would cut and bring into the house a huge green log, an 'all-nighter'. The fire would be raked and scattered and the big log placed on the embers. The log would then smoulder gently all night long and the cook in charge would only have to spend ten or fifteen minutes in the morning with dry twigs and split kindling, blowing and fanning until it flared bright and hot to cook the breakfast of boiled wheat and cereal coffee.

But nights were not entirely peaceful. There was a pile of pea straw still stacked in one of the storage bays and all night long this pea stack jumped and squealed with rats.

I found a group of villagers one morning, squatting outside the back door of the round house with a great pile of pea haulm in front of them, sorting through the straw and picking off the dry pods. Little Pete and Nick Ainsworth, helped spasmodically by Robin, were dragging more heaps of haulm out of the house.

'It's been keeping Sharon awake,' said Jill, by way of explanation. 'Not the peas, the rats. Sharon can now identify each rat in there by its own little voice, she assures us, and she would like them to go away and leave her alone, but they won't listen to her.'

'Yes, Marmaduke and Oswald and Horatio and lots of other rats . . .' added Sharon, giggling.

'As far as Sharon's concerned, anything's a rat that moves,' commented John Rossetti.

'That's not true,' protested Sharon. 'It's just that you don't live on my side, so you just don't know.'

'Anyway, the rats are eating all the peas,' said Martin, 'and they're eating all the wheat as well, at a very fast rate. So we're going to thresh all the wheat and put it in a rat proof container.'

Eventually they did, but first they had to remove all the offending peas and store them in a barrel. The pea straw they stuffed into the raised storage 'granaries' they had built to hold the wheat, so they found a use for them after all. The pea straw later came in handy as extra forage for the animals.

On December the fourth, Brigid, the only cow with a Celtic name, finally calved. She was the animal who had been so wretchedly infected with warbles earlier in the year and even then she had been in calf with the little Highland cross heifer she now produced. The villagers had been half hoping for a bull calf so that they could kill it and have the rennet for cheese making, but instead they all quickly fell in love with Rosie, the little heifer. She was a pretty creature with a thick curly coat the colour of dark chocolate, huge brown eyes and long, seductive eyelashes. They spoiled her totally.

Out in the field Pete Ainsworth and Pete Little had got two of the other cows, Betsy and Jacky, yoked to the plough and had begun to cut the first furrows in the stubbled ground. Most of the time Pete Little led the cows, with a rope halter on one of them, crying instructions and encouragement. 'Go right, Jacky, right, Betsy, good girl, good girl.'

The cows strained at the yoke; Betsy, who was much the heavier animal, made heavier weather of the work. The men rested the cows after every ten furrows and never worked more than forty furrows at a time.

Pete Ainsworth did the actual ploughing, wrestling with the ard which he had made himself. The iron tip carved long, uneven scratches a few inches into the earth, turning up the weeds that had already taken root in the wet days following the harvest. It was difficult to get the furrows running straight and the earth turned sufficiently to kill the weeds and prepare a tilth for the following spring. How the Iron Age farmers solved this problem is not entirely clear. Whole fields unploughed since Iron Age times have now been excavated intact and the scratches in the chalk subsoil show rather wavy parallel lines, about a foot apart, running at right angles and criss-crossing the field like primitive graph paper. At first sight this would suggest that the Celtic farmers were satisfied with furrows spaced this far apart, but other excavations have also shown that the headlands, the corners and field edges left unploughed where the

Peter Little and Jill ploughing with the cows.

beasts were turned, were dug by hand with that most English of digging instruments, a spade. The iron rims of metal shod wooden spades turn up quite frequently on Iron Age excavations in Britain and the use of a spade in this way implies intensive, careful cultivation. I myself now believe that the Celts probably understood the necessity for sub-soiling, breaking up the plough pan of hard earth that forms under the surface of any cultivated land at the normal depth of cultivation. If they knew about this they might have ploughed at a depth of three or four inches for, say, three furrows and much deeper for the fourth and so on, across the field. Alternatively, they may have ploughed the deep, widely-spaced furrows only once every five or ten seasons, when poor crops indicated that the plough pan needed breaking up.

At any event, the two Petes found that even with criss-cross ploughing, the ground was not sufficiently turned to break down to a fine tilth, even after the winter frosts. In fact the solution they later adopted was to plough again and again at intervals throughout the winter until the ground was ready for the seed in spring, but Iron Age farmers are known to have grown a great deal of Spelt, a winter wheat which needs to be sown in the autumn. Peter Reynolds at the Butser Ancient Farm has grown successful crops of this grain for several seasons, but the scale of operation is still too small to judge whether the techniques he uses are correct. Hand hoeing for instance, though some adzes could have been used as small hoes, is not really justified by the archaeological record. The mystery remains.

Pete Ainsworth was also working on the frame of a cart. He had selected a young ash tree with a deep Y fork, some fifteen feet off the ground, felled the tree and axed most of the surplus wood. Now he was working with an adze to make the rough surfaces smooth. Later, the Y part of the frame would be supported by an axle underneath and the floor planks of the cart would be secured to the top. The long stem of the Y would carry the yoke for the cows. Carts of this pattern have cropped up in bogs and burials at various sites in Europe and some have even survived in country districts to the present day. Pete was working with an eye to the future. He knew that the cart would take many weeks to finish and might well not be complete until the spring, but the Ainsworths had settled down. Lindsay was dyeing raw wool in a tub of yew chips, preparatory to the long process of spinning and weaving it into cloth. It seemed that they were determined to stick it out to the end and the customary sniping and sighing over Lindsay's waywardness had been in abeyance since the big rows of the previous month. Then a situation arose that brought the whole question of their leaving to the fore once again. Nick's rectal prolapse returned.

Nick himself reported the fact, without much concern. Martin rectified the prolapse without difficulty but he could see that Pete and Lindsay were worried and recommended me to call in the local general practitioner. This doctor, when he examined Nick, was very reassuring, but he offered to make an appointment with a specialist paediatrician at a nearby hospital, if they were not entirely satisfied. So one afternoon Linda brought the Ainsworths some reasonably presentable modern clothes and, complete with film crew, we trooped into the local hospital, about twenty miles away. Nick was delighted by the expedition, excited by the sights and sounds of the modern world and overjoyed with the books and toys in the children's waiting room. He certainly did not look ill, but his parents were plainly tense and worried.

The specialist's report was equivocal, but within twelve hours the Ainsworths were preparing to leave the project. 'The specialist said he didn't necessarily have to have an operation yet,' Lindsay explained, 'and he didn't think it would make it any worse for Nick to stay here for the remaining three months, but we discussed it afterwards and we felt that we weren't doing anything positive about it by staying here.'

'Yes, we've no qualms about the project . . . or the conditions here . . .' agreed Pete. 'It's just that we would be a lot happier in our own minds if we could get him home.'

Lindsay had great faith in her own preferred diet of abundant fresh fruit and fruit juices to help Nick's digestive processes. By this time there was no fresh fruit of any kind to be had in the village and to bring it in would have been a distortion of the whole project. There was also the problem of the toilet facilities. The pit latrine was a good thirty yards from the back entrance of the round house and the journey by night involved negotiating a route round the store hut and steering clear of an open pit about eight feet deep, close to the latrine.

A few nights before Pete Ainsworth had been carrying Robin to the latrine and had fallen into the pit en route. Fortunately, Robin had been thrown clear, but Pete had hurt his arm quite badly in the fall and understandably did not relish the idea of Nick doing likewise. The alternative to the latrine was squatting in the mud, not a process recommended to a child with a rectal prolapse. Any parents might well have felt the same about their small son in the same circumstances. The remarkable thing really was not that the Ainsworths were now determined to leave, but that they had stuck the project for so long.

Arrangements were quickly made for their departure. Pete's mother and father came down with a car to take them home. There was a press conference and the story of Nick's intractable bowels was spread around the world. The Ainsworths swiftly adapted back to life in the twentieth century and within a few weeks the children were back at school, happily scoffing at their nine-month adventure as 'the silly time', thus neatly avoiding the envy of their schoolfriends. But in the Iron Age village the children were sadly missed. They had given life to the place and also a kind of authenticity, the feeling, as Sarah put it, that they were all one big family. Without the children there were no dependent beings, just a team of fit young adults, a far more artificial community. At the same time the group were also profoundly relieved. The whole atmosphere of the place relaxed, unwound, and a new harmony existed in the village.

As though to celebrate freedom from vegetarian scruples the villagers killed the young steer the same week. Meat was everywhere. Great slabs of fillet steak broiled on sticks over the fire. Huge haunches hung from the roof beams or sat pickling in barrels, and the cauldron seemed to be perpetually bubbling with soup. For several days they did not bother to bake bread or eat boiled wheat. They had an orgy of meat-eating instead.

A day or two after the steer had been butchered, Sharon decided to make some bone broth. She groped in the wooden buckets in the dark and came up with some meaty bones and soon they were simmering away in the cauldron. Anxious to get a nice clear beef soup she then strained the bones and scraps of meat through a cloth, served up the consommé and chucked the bones to the pigs.

In the morning Sarah, who had done most of the work of butchering the carcase, came to take stock of the meat supply.

'Hey, where's that meat got to that was in this bucket?'

'Was it meat with bones in it?' asked Sharon.

'Well yes,' replied Sarah, puzzled. 'A bit of the spine with one or two little ribs.'

'Oh, that's all right then,' said Sharon cheerfully. 'I made soup out of it and then chucked the bits to the pigs.'

'Then they're very lucky pigs,' responded Sarah with some asperity. 'That, my dear Sharon, was sirloin steak!'

The meat supply was certainly abundant. They had the steer and there was also Mary, the old Dexter who was not long for this world and would eventually end up on the table; they also intended to eat two of the four little pigs which were still in the pens, and they had several lambs still to consume. But one cold dark night their plans for the sheep received a setback.

It was Sharon's job at this time to look after the sheep. Every day she filled two baskets with hay from the stacks, carried them to the field and called the sheep over to eat the fodder. There should have been twelve Soays in the field and thirteen Shetlands, but there were only eight of the little brown Soays eating hay that morning. Sharon blinked and peered around the field, puzzled, but not unduly worried. The Soays quite frequently got out of the field and trotted off through the woods in search of better pasture. Later that week the Soay ram jumped out, travelled a mile and a half to a field full of fat downland ewes and ran amok amongst them, like a small brown rapist in a nunnery. He was recaptured, as the Soays always were, by determined Iron Age sheep trackers. So Sharon went back to the round house, reported the loss and the sheep trackers went out to look for them.

'Actually I was sceptical at first because Sharon is a bit short-sighted,' explained John Rossetti later, 'and the Soays usually escape all together or not at all, but sure enough, there were four missing.'

They cast around, searching for clues, and to their surprise found fresh tyre marks by the gate to the forest track. Close to the field entrance was a pool of frothy blood and there were dogs' paw prints in the soft earth. It seemed impossible, but there was every sign that the Soays had been rustled, run down with dogs, butchered and carried away. Deer poaching is known to be big business. Venison fetches up to two pounds per pound weight on the restaurant black market, and men with trained lurcher dogs hunt ruthlessly and silently, making their escape in vehicles stolen for the occasion. Perhaps out of luck with the deer, poachers had turned their dogs on the sheep instead, or they may even have mistaken the fleet-footed Soays for roe deer in the darkness. It probably made no difference to the dogs, anyway.

The villagers were philosophical about it. 'Put it down to wolves or raiders from another tribe,' said Jill, who loved to indulge a free-ranging imagination.

'I don't envy them eating those Soays,' Sarah remarked, 'three of them were really ancient, all skin and bone.'

'Oh well,' said John Rossetti, philosophically, 'once they've tried eating them I don't suppose they'll be back for more!'

Eating and drinking became almost orgiastic in the village over the next week. The group had decided to celebrate the winter solstice, the shortest day, on December the twenty-first in preference to Christmas, because of course they were supposed to be living in a pre-Christian environment – not that they fooled themselves about that, but the game of celebrating the pagan festivals helped them to put up with the privations of life on the project.

Martin explained: 'Well, obviously we couldn't have Christmas and thought we'd have Solstice instead. So we've decided we're having Solstice Eve and Solstice Day and Solstice Boxing Day . . .'

They decked the house with Solstice decorations, holly and ivy, the only reminders of summer life still green in the woods, and of course mistletoe, that mythic Celtic plant that everyone associates with Druidic rites. 'I won't be able to enjoy it without mistletoe,' Martin asserted loudly.

On Solstice Eve they built a big bonfire outside the palisade in the same spot where they had burned the Wicker Man. To this party they invited a number of people from the surrounding estate.

Although they had been cut off almost completely from the outside world there were a number of forest workers with whom they inevitably came in touch from time to time. There was the deerkeeper and his wife, the pheasant keeper, the farmer who had let his field to them, a schoolteacher and his wife who lived in a cottage on the far side of the woods, and one or two others. Throughout the year these people had been very kind, not least in the way that they avoided too close a contact with the settlement, exchanging friendly greetings if they met in the woods, but usually leaving it at that. There had been one or two bits of friendly cheating – a surreptitious gift of cakes on the night of the Queen's Jubilee, a couple of hares draped prominently over an ineffective Iron Age trap. There might have been far more of these gifts if the villagers had not adopted a conscientious puritanism about them.

All these people were now invited to a party on Solstice Eve. The villagers proudly served them with roast goose and roast beef, black pudding and lactic cheese and beautifully plaited loaves of bread baked specially for the occasion. They also plied their guests with liberal quantities of elderberry wine. In return they received more contraband hares, several bottles of modern wine and, most prized of all, twelve potatoes wrapped in foil, ready to be baked in the embers of the fire. Later, when they were grilled by pressmen, the villagers stolidly denied that there had been any cheating and I endorsed them in this. The cheats there were have now been confessed. They do not amount to very much.

A day of festivities was followed by another. On the evening of Solstice Day itself they placed small clay lamps all round the interior of the round house. It was interesting to see the effect of these. They were very simple, nothing more than shallow saucers of baked clay with linen wicks floating in a pool of lard. Had there been a more plentiful supply of animal fat they could have had the lamps lit every night, but the amount of extra light they added to the interior of the round house was negligible compared with the light from the fire itself. By this time, in any case, the villagers had become expert at living in darkness, doing many simple jobs and finding their way about by touch alone. If they were anxious to find something they would take a handful of twisted straw, light it from the fire and use it as an improvised torch. The little clay lamps were nowhere near as bright, but what they did was to lend a delightful festive atmosphere to the inside of the house. Look no further for the significance of Christmas candles and fairy lights. Poor people can afford lights only for festivals.

For some days each person in the group had been 'secretly' making a Solstice present for someone else. All these gifts were now hidden in a large basket full of hay with long strings attached to each gift. Martin, loudly maintaining that he was Father Solstice, carried the basket to the fireside and each person in turn, beginning with the youngest, had a random chance at the basket. The presents illustrated the range of skills they were beginning to acquire. Kate got a little clay figurine, an emblematic 'Mother Goddess', Helen a sprang bag, Martin a small carved wooden medallion, Sarah a boar's tusk, mounted in cold beaten bronze, and so on round the group.

To a plaintive and slightly uncertain tune, played by Kate on a wooden recorder made by her husband John, the party got under way. There was more roast beef turning deliciously on a spit over the fire and more elderberry wine. I remember very little about the evening except that I was ill and woke up in the morning wrapped in sheepskin in the Ainsworths' recently vacted bed chamber.

By Christmas time the Iron Age festivities were over and the village had gone back to work. The crafts which had produced the Solstice presents now occupied a great deal of everybody's time. Music was one of the joys of modern living which they missed most of all, and several people had tried their hands at making musical instruments. John Rossetti succeeded in making a crude wooden recorder, and Brian, who was probably the most skilled craftsman on the project, was now making a wooden lyre with exquisite care. This was based on a medieval pattern, but the lyre is one of the most ancient of all stringed instruments, with strong affinities to the Celtic world.

Weaving was also far more sophisticated in prehistoric times than the technology first suggests, as the girls came to understand as they worked on the loom. They were also making more baskets, spinning

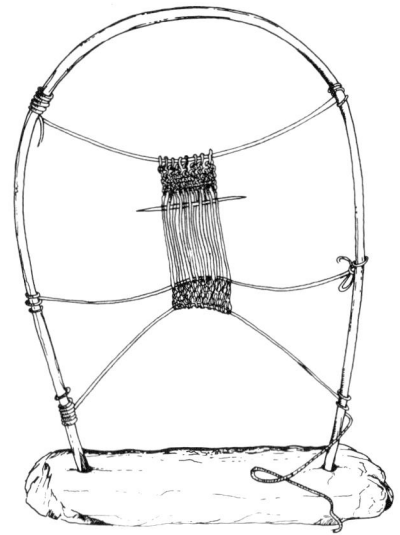

Sprang frame.

and knitting more and more of their own clothes and working on the sprang frame. This, too, is an ancient craft, practised in varying forms in many different countries. The basic principle is rather like the child's game of cat's cradle, when strings are twisted and looped together under tension to produce a complex interwoven pattern. Because, unlike knitting or crochet, the threads have to be kept taut, sprang is made on a frame, and theirs consisted of an overbent bow of hazel secured to a heavier wooden base. The great advantage of a bag made of sprang is that the technique gives the woollen threads elasticity. The bag can expand to hold things stuffed into it and collapse again afterwards, more or less back to its original shape.

The men, as a rule, practised different crafts from the women. This was partly a reflection of the choices they made in the training period of preparation for the project and partly of course the effect of their whole experience of life. Martin had made a conscious choice and learned as much as he could about bronze casting before he came. Bronze of course is the precursor of iron in the history of metallurgy. By Iron Age times it was used in Britain mainly for decorative work and bronze mirrors and ceremonial shields of great beauty have been recovered from graves and river beds, where they may have been placed as ritual offerings. Martin could not hope to match the skill of the prehistoric bronze smiths, but he did want to master the basic techniques. He prepared small triangular crucibles, identical to those found on Iron Age sites, and made himself a small bowl furnace, very similar to the blacksmiths', but more enclosed, with semicircular walls of clay which helped to build up the heat. He also prepared moulds, again almost identical to Iron Age examples.

'First you've got to make a wax model of what you want,' he explained. 'This is a model for a penanular brooch.'

He held up a little ring of beeswax, the circle broken in the middle to take a retaining pin. 'Then you've got to attach a runner, a model of the channel which the molten bronze will have to run down, with a little reservoir at the top. Then you encase the whole thing in clay, using a very finely grogged clay and press it on tight to get the detail and then you put a wrap-over layer of coarser clay over that and you end up with a mould. Then you wait for it to dry out, bung it in the fire in the evening and fire it. Of course the wax melts and runs out and you're left with a hole inside the mould which is the shape of the thing you want.'

Martin placed a crucible containing some fragments of bronze in the furnace and popped the mould into a slightly cooler part of the fire. The tuyère on Martin's furnace directed the draught directly down on top of the crucible holding the bronze. It was possible to watch the heat building up as he worked, his face streaked where streams of sweat had made miniature water courses through the grime from the charcoal dust. Each woosh of the bellows made a miniature explosion of sparks and the charcoal fire shrank visibly. 'You use a fair bit of charcoal doing this,' he panted, and heaped fresh lumps into the furnace.

After about twenty minutes of strenuous work the bronze had melted and he was ready for the pour. With frenzied haste, to ensure that the bronze stayed molten, he raked away the glowing charcoal, seized the crucible in a pair of blacksmith's tongs, knocked the cap off the mould and poured the white hot metal into the funnel at the top. 'Now you have to wait for the perishing thing to cool,' Martin announced, and sank into an exhausted heap on the earth floor.

When he came to break off the clay mould with careful blows from a hammer the brooch was revealed as a faithful copy of the wax original, but there were tiny fragments of charcoal embedded in the metal. 'I wonder how that happened,' muttered Martin. 'I thought we'd beaten that problem. Oh well, better than last time. Next time, better still.'

It was a philosophy that the two Johns, the blacksmiths, also endorsed. They, too, were slowly becoming more skilled after long hours of work, pumping the bellows and wielding the hammer sometimes late into the evening. To their delight they succeeded in building up enough heat to weld iron, hammering two almost molten surfaces together so that they stayed together. But welding had its disadvantages. As the hammer slammed down on the white hot iron an impressive shower of molten metal sprayed in all directions in a spectacular display of primeval fireworks, but molten metal on bare skin is no joke and more than once the sparks flew while someone was in the bath. After loud and angry protests from burned villagers the blacksmiths adopted an early warning system. 'We're going to do a weld,' John Rockliff would announce in deafening tones. 'Now!' he shouted and fireside bathers and basket makers scattered in all directions as the sizzling sparks began to fly.

But of all the crafts, the one most in demand was the art of the shoemaker. As the winter rain poured steadily down on the settlement the mud around the palisade got relentlessly deeper. At certain critical points, on the path to the well for instance, they laid down hurdles in the mud to help provide a relatively dry footing. On the

John Rossetti turning wood on the pole lathe . . .

. . . and working with a draw knife on the vice.

path to the main entrance to the palisade Brian laid a causeway of flint. John Rossetti and many others from time to time cut drainage channels through the worst of the mire in an effort to reduce the surface water, but mud was everywhere, wet, sticky, and bitterly cold on unprotected feet.

'People may imagine you get used to it, getting cold feet, I mean,' remarked Sarah one wet and windy day, as her bare toes squidged through the mud in the compound. 'But you don't. Cold feet are still cold feet.'

Sarah had discarded her shoes, not out of masochism, but because they were soaked through and it was generally agreed that wet shoes were even more miserable than bare feet, because they took longer to warm up again. The solution was pattens, separate soles of wood, platforms for the feet, fixed by a variety of methods to the underside of the leather shoes. All the villagers developed a slow, trudging, flat-footed walk to cope with the unyielding pattens and the slippery mire.

'You just can't imagine what it's like having to wade through it,' said Sarah. 'I mean, in the middle of the night you want to go to the loo and you think,' she laughed, 'you think "I'll hold on a bit longer" because you've got to face the mud. And then you've got to grope in the dark to find something to put on your feet. It's terrible, it really is.'

I could not fully appreciate the problem, because I always wore thick rubber boots on the site, but I could not help noticing that whenever I spent a night in the round house and took my boots off before climbing into a sheepskin blanket, my boots were never in the same place in the morning. They walked, many times over, in the night.

Chapter Fourteen

By January the stacks of stored grain were rapidly diminishing. The wheat had almost all been threshed and stored out of reach of the rats in sacks and barrels. The villagers processed the barley by pulling off the heads so that the pigs would find the grain more easily, but they did not bother to thresh it except for malting to make beer. Oats were used exclusively for animal fodder because the job of removing the husk from the grain was virtually impossible to perform except on a very small scale. But the rats had attacked all three cereals, and the barley stack still harboured a great number of them. So one bright cold morning the villagers decided to wreak vengeance.

They assembled their armament of heavy sticks and enlisted additional storm troops in the shape of Siri the lurcher and the three polecats. Then they began to take the barley stack apart, sheaf by sheaf. The first find was a nest of baby mice which brought some sentimental *oohs!* and *ahs!* from the girls but the animals were ruthlessly set aside as polecat food. Then, as they neared the bottom of the stack, the rats began to jump. A kind of frenzy seems to have taken over with sticks flailing, the dog leaping and rats flying in all directions. Siri, with marvellous dexterity, killed rats in mid-air, on the stack and under it, somehow managing to discriminate between the rats and the polecats, which were writhing invisibly under the last sheaves of straw. Sarah, not usually noted for her bloodthirsty nature, was seizing maimed rats by the tail and smashing them against a post. Kate stamped one to death beneath her high-heeled patten. Even Helen, usually the gentlest of creatures, got caught up in the hunt. The count, at the end of the blood orgy, was seventy-five dead rats neatly laid out on a hurdle as trophies of the chase.

John Rossetti fingered a plump rat carcass, grown fat on the precious wheat and barley. The following day he skewered three of the plumpest specimens and he and John Rockcliff spit-roast them over the fire so that everyone could eat a few morsels of roasted rat.

'It's not that bad,' said Helen, but she ate only a fragment as an act of collective solidarity.

'Rather like lamb,' said Sarah thoughtfully, 'but a bit dry!'

'Better than lamb,' insisted John Rossetti, 'but not as succulent as squirrel.'

'There's not a great deal of meat on a rat though,' said Martin. 'I mean, you wouldn't grow fat on rat, would you?'

The rats continued to be a problem, but one they could control to some extent by taking great care with the storage of food, and in this respect it was not just the rats they had to worry about. One winter day the group acquired a deer. It had got entangled in some fencing on the forest edge and they put it out of misery with a well-aimed blow from a mallet. The carcass was toted back to the village and hung high in the rafters of the small storage hut. During the night the big mongrel Emer, not normally the most athletic of dogs, leaped high enough to reach it and pull it to the ground. Philosophically, they re-hung what was left of the carcass even higher from the ground, but a night or two later Emer broke into the storage hut again and this time consumed the lot.

'Just think of it,' said John Rossetti, with grudging respect, 'two days' meat for ten people eaten in two nights by one dog!'

But they were not usually short of meat. Sharon had been a beans and brown rice freak before the project and she was much given to oriental philosophy and the mystique of a wholefood diet. The controversy over meat eating and the hunger for meat which had now overtaken all of them prompted her to reflect on some of the peculiarities of Iron Age economics as practised by the group. 'The thing is that we're always being told these days that it saves energy if you eat vegetable protein direct rather than letting an animal process it for you. You know, it takes ten pounds of vegetable protein to make one pound of beef and all that. . . .' She paused, trying to formulate the thought in her mind. Sharon was often thoughtful but not always completely coherent. 'Well, look at the amount of energy it takes for us to turn wheat into flour. You know, cutting the wheat, threshing, winnowing, pounding, grinding and then all the business of baking our bread . . . Well, it's a lot easier for us just to feed the unthreshed grain to the animals and then to slaughter them.'

But for all their apparently casual attitude to animal slaughter, the villagers enjoyed extraordinarily close relationships to animals. There was Gloria, for instance, the pig who liked to be tickled. Gloria was ginger in colour, more like an ordinary Tamworth pig than a wild boar, and no bars could hold her. She had learned the trick of leaping over the wall of the pig pen, and leaving brothers and sister behind her, she acquainted herself with the world of human beings. She would wander in and out of the house, stealing food if there was any around to be stolen, snuffing round clothes, leaping on and off beds, teasing the dogs and provoking people. She particularly liked Brian and would follow him around like a dog, poking her snout into whatever he happened to be doing at the time. This was partly cupboard love, because Brian was pig keeper, but also sheer sensual delight. If Brian stroked her she would quiver with pleasure, then roll over on her back with her legs in the air, an expression of purest ecstasy on her fat, piggy face. Everybody knew that Gloria would one day be killed, not in some anonymous abattoir, but by them and for them.

Brian would mutter culinary endearments as he stroked her tummy. 'Going to make nice bacon, then?' he would say, as he nudged her in the ribs. To the sensitive outsider, reared on the Muppets' school of animal husbandry, this might seem unbelievably callous, but even in ten short months the villagers had learned to be realistic about animals, never cruel, never even unnecessarily brusque in handling them, but always with an eye on the end product, meat. Gloria's own attitude more than matched theirs. The film crew were recording one day the capture and slaughter of a lamb. With practised skill John Rockliff and Martin killed it and hung it from the branch of a tree to complete the butchering process. As they dumped the guts in a bucket, Gloria snuffled at their feet, trying to grab a morsel of raw meat or drink the blood from the bucket. When the opportunity arose she raised her bloody snout and tried to tear a lump from the headless carcass: pigs, like human beings, can be carnivores.

The skins from the animals went to Helen for processing. In her quiet way she had made quite a lot of progress in the tanning trade, working hard at a job which no one else seemed to want to do. With a draw knife she had scraped large quantities of bark from the oak trees around the clearing and steeped the bark shavings in a tub of water. After several weeks of steeping, the water was a rich brown. 'Oak bark is very rich in tannins, you see,' Helen explained. 'One of the techniques for a quick tan is to hang the skin up like a bag, with the tanning solution inside it, but the shape of the skin just isn't right for it, so I suspended it in a puddle of oak bark liquid and I'm hoping the stuff will just soak through the skin.' She laughed. 'It smells all right, anyway.'

So far, no one had used skins for clothing except Sarah, who had a back warmer of hare's fur, to stop the winter aches and pains from which she suffered, and Jill and Kate, who both had smart fur hats which made them look a bit like comrade delegates to the Astrakhan People's Congress. The peasant look was accentuated by the new woven garments that began to make their appearance. Jill had a full length cloak, fashioned from material she had woven herself, complete with a hood. Jill did not know it, but the cape was almost uncannily similar to the cloaks so clearly shown on a Celtic votive stone from Housesteads in Northumberland which depicts three hooded figures. Jill's cape, which had taken up almost the full length and width of the loom, was heavy, warm, and cunningly striped with different vegetable dyes.

Sarah had finally persuaded her husband John to complete a second loom which was now set up at the rear entrance to the house. He would have finished it before but he had got carried away doing pretty poker-work designs on the uprights. On this Sarah had woven a rather smaller piece of cloth than Jill's, which had not taken up the full width of the loom.

'I want it to, but it won't,' complained Sarah. 'It's got a will of its own.' Once the woven piece was complete she sat, curled up on the floor by the fire, sewing the fabric together. 'Look, it's shrunk terribly now I've washed it,' she said. 'It's going to be the only Iron Age mini skirt ever recorded.' Patiently, she plied the bone needle. 'Needles are very precious here,' she explained. 'It's a number one sin to lose a needle because it takes the best part of a morning to make one. And sewing's sort of different because there are no scissors . . . I mean I have to cut the thread with a knife. And there are no pins to hold it together. You just have to hope,' she laughed. The linen thread she was using kept snapping, and each time this happened, she had to stop sewing, knot the thread, and begin all over again.

'How long do you think the whole process of making that skirt will take, from beginning to end?' I asked.

'What, beginning with shearing the sheep?' she laughed again. 'Well, first you've got to dye the wool and that means going out and finding the lichens and the ash bark to dye it with. Then you've got to spin the wool, that's ten or eleven balls of wool this size.' She held up a ball the size of a grapefruit. 'They were all plied, two ply, and that's a lot of evenings' spinning. Then there's setting up the loom, which took the best part of two days just to get the warp threads arranged. Just how long the weaving took is difficult to say because I only did it in fits and starts. Then there's the sewing, and you have to spin the linen thread as well. And you may have to make another needle if the one you were going to use is lost. Oh, I should think this one skirt will take about a month's work from beginning to end.'

Even allowing for much greater skill on the part of the weaver it was difficult to imagine how the process could be cut down by more than say thirty-three per cent, which would make the equation one skirt to twenty days' work. But the work was seasonal. Spinning went on throughout the year. Dyeing was done in the autumn and weaving in the winter, and all these tasks were fitted in with other jobs. Moreover, as Jill pointed out, the clothes they made were extremely strong and durable. By the end of the project Jill was skilled enough to manage a number of different weaving techniques on the simple loom. She could produce, for instance, handsome seamless tubes of cloth for trouser legs. The girls were in no doubt that they could make enough clothes for everybody for an indefinite length of time, given that they had enough wool and sufficient sheep to provide it.

Although one or two of the men did have a try at weaving and although Pete Little and John Rockliff spent many hours spinning, making clothes was very much women's work, just as blacksmithing was men's work. Pottery, eventually, was shared by everyone, though Martin and Brian remained the master potters. The continued division of labour prompted me to ask Jill and Pete if they felt that women were still being discriminated against in any sphere of activity.

'Well it depends what you mean,' said Pete, ruefully. 'I mean, I much more often go and chop the wood on cooking days and bring it in and fire the oven than Jill does.'

This was, in fact, the common pattern on the project. Women, on the other hand, almost invariably kneaded the dough for the bread.

'Yes that's a difficult one,' admitted Jill. 'Because there's so much of how you've been brought up in it. And if you've made the bread last week it's easier to make the bread this week, because all the time we're learning how to do these jobs better. Sometimes I make a point of changing around, but then I find I have to ask Pete . . . how do you block the door of the oven or something. . . .' she paused, thoughtfully. 'I think it's laziness really,' she announced. 'I mean, I think women are very lazy. It's so much easier to send someone to the well than to do it yourself.'

'Yes, we're a weak lot, we men,' said Pete with a laugh. 'We don't stand up for our rights at all.'

Jill interrupted him. 'Well I don't know if it's nagging or what, but it does seem that the female element has quite a dominant voice over the things that go on here. I do believe we've got a bit of a matriarchy.'

When I thought about it this seemed to me to be true. It was the women who were in command of the domestic process, the cooking, the washing-up, the daily round of many of the household jobs. And although the men had many skilled tasks, specialist jobs which they more or less monopolised, women rarely had scruples about interrupting them and sending them off literally to hew wood and draw water. But masculine subservience was not a matter of simple weakness. The point was that there was no escape from the settlement, no male sphere of activity away from home that the men could make entirely their own. In Iron Age times no doubt hunting or fighting or even the heavy demands of intensive agriculture would have removed the men from the house most of the time, while the women would have been burdened with children and the drain on health and energy that multiple childbirth often entails. On the project, Lindsay apart, the women had no such burdens, only the pattern of domestic matriarchy that rules in so many households in the western world, when the men return from their excursions into the outside world. In the home the women rule, and on the project there was nowhere else to go.

Towards the end of January there was the first heavy fall of snow. The villagers woke up one morning to a new world. The black twigs of the trees around the clearing were outlined in shiny white. Snow hung thick on the conical roofs, but not for long on the great roof of the big round house, which was soon steaming brown again as the fires within melted it bare. Excited, the villagers made footprints in the snow, delighted by the different texture beneath their feet.

John Rockcliff, faced with a problem, cogitated deeply and came up with a solution. 'Barrel staves,' he announced.

Enlightened, the villagers equipped themselves with the long curved wooden staves from broken barrels and gathered at the top of the long slope which led from the clearing near the field entrance to the deep valley below. The path was thickly coated with snow which soon compacted down to make a splendid toboggan run. Down they rode, some teetering on two staves at once, constantly in danger of doing the splits, some riding on a single stave with legs gathered beneath them. Soon the braver spirits were lying full length and scorching down the slope with all the riotous enthusiasm of children in a school playground. There were grazed hands and bruised limbs, but no serious damage as villager after villager tumbled head over heels at the bottom of the slope.

They could not go on long because of the myriad jobs which always demanded to be done, so they waited until the day's work was finished and came back after supper in the evening. The moon was bright that night and they tobogganed by moonlight, shouting and laughing in the still, silvery air.

But this was a rare night excursion. In January the round house door was usually closed by six o'clock. During these short days of winter I often made my daily visit to the village in the evening and joined the group gathered round the fire. Although most people would be doing something with their hands, they always found time to talk. Conversation was not scintillating. Often they would discuss plans for the future, places where they would go, holidays they planned to take, once the project was over. Some of the girls, Jill, Kate and Sharon particularly, had a habit of trying to recall the words of a song or the plot of a book, always maddeningly incomplete in the memory. Sometimes, too often perhaps, they would become aware that they had almost exactly the same conversation before, exchanging almost the same words.

Occasionally they would become aware that their intellectual muscles were out of training, as it were, and they would try and have a serious conversation about some idea or belief which had preoccupied them in their ordinary lives. But conversations like this never thrived. They quickly became aware how little they had in common. Sarah and John, for instance, were both Christians while the rest of the group were more or less agnostic. Others differed in their political convictions, or, like Martin, insisted on taking the opposite point of view just for the sake of the argument. The things that tied them together were far more cogent and far more immediate. They now knew each other so well that they employed a kind of verbal shorthand. They were quite sharply critical of one another in a way that none of them would have dared a few months before, and if someone stepped out of line, he or she would often experience the full weight of collective disapproval. To me, as an outsider, however often I visited and however long I stayed, this private language and the force it carried remained always something of a mystery. But there was no mistaking a mood in the group.

If there was anger in the air, or depression, or if there had simply been an unpleasant row between individuals, the effect was almost tangible. I could feel it immediately I entered the house and would then have to set to work, slowly, to try to establish exactly what was going on. But the great joy of those January evenings was that the mood was almost always mellow, affectionate, reaching out and embracing all of them.

Nevertheless, there were still minor frustrations. 'There's so little scope for rebellious feelings in this situation,' John Rossetti explained. 'Most of us are people who are used to doing our own thing, but we're stuck in a situation where there are very strict rules of living and the rules are very much made by ourselves and we know we have to conform to those rules otherwise the whole point of the project disappears . . . it's a terrible feeling really. You feel you can't rebel against the authority because you are the authority. You really feel you want to break out and go down to the pub or something or, you know, just scream at the top of your voice.'

John Rockliff nodded agreement.

'What about leadership?' I asked. 'Lots of people I talk to about this project imagine that you must have a leader.'

'No we don't,' said Sarah, with a smile.

'Definitely not,' said Martin, with rather more vehemence.

'We don't need one,' added Sarah.

'How do you arrive at decisions then?'

'Oh, we like arguing.'

John Rossetti came back into the discussion: 'Not only do we not need a leader, but we couldn't actually support one. I mean we're all so much at the same level, so much of the same age and if somebody did put himself up front they wouldn't last very long.'

So the group continued to solve their problems, not so much by committee perhaps, as by collectively following what seemed the best idea at the time. When one of the villagers had demonstrated convincingly that they had acquired expertise in one field, their opinion was respected by everyone else. Jill, for example, was the acknowledged expert on weaving and basketwork, and the other girls would consult her in these areas. But even those, like Brian, who never entered into a debate with the verbal dexterity of Martin or Jill would often assert themselves in action rather than words, and be as frequently followed. Pete Little, who had quietly got on with the job of making the cart where Pete Ainsworth had abandoned it, was eventually followed by all the men in the project as they helped him to complete it.

The cart took shape slowly, in pieces, and it seemed to me that only Pete, and later Brian, fully understood how it was eventually to be put together. The wheels in themselves were complex. Pete took six enormous blocks of oak and fashioned them by axe and adze into sections which fitted together with oak dowel rods like a gigantic child's toy. The dexterity with which he and Brian worked with the

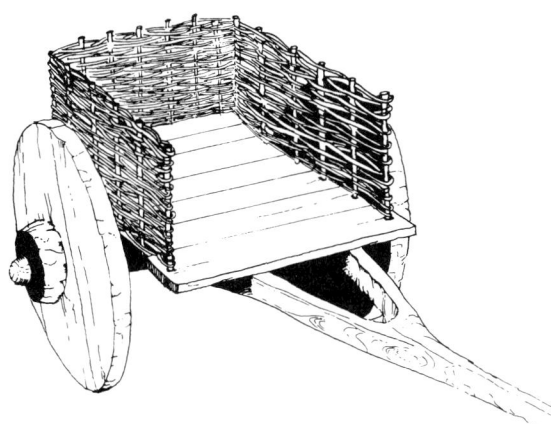

The finished cart.

clumsy iron tools never ceased to amaze me. Each wheel was in three parts. The central piece in each one incorporated a huge central hub to take the axle and tapered down to a much thinner rim, only about five inches thick, which was curved at the edge to form the central part of a circle about three foot six in diameter. The two outer sections were tailored to complete the circle, exactly matching the centre piece. I could not believe it was possible to work freehand with a heavy adze with such finesse that all the sections would marry together, but they did, with amazing accuracy. However, even as Pete and Brian accomplished this feat they simply nodded together, quietly, in calm accord.

The two Johns were still busy at the forge. They were trying to make a pair of iron firedogs, replicas of the great iron frames on which the Iron Age aristocrats turned their great roasts of pork and beef. This, like the cart, was a complex technical exercise, demanding several welds at key points of the construction, difficult to achieve because of the small size of the furnace at their disposal and the even smaller size of the 'hot spot' in the centre of the fire. The raw material they had to work with was in the form of 'sword' ingots. These have been recovered from many Iron Age sites, especially in southern Britain. Typically they are between two and three feet long, flat in section and shaped roughly like a sword with a tubular handle instead of a hilt. The two Johns took a dim view of these ingots and John Rockliff, as usual, had a theory about them.

'We've been wondering why they were so long and thin and really pretty useless for making lots of things, and we thought maybe it was some sort of restrictive practice that blacksmiths had in the Iron Age – that they didn't want everybody copying their highly paid craft so they

Fitting the wheels to the axle of the cart.

turned their iron into this shape so that only a very skilled blacksmith could knock it back together and make something useful out of it.'

He demonstrated how each ingot would have to be folded and welded, folded and welded, in order to make something solid like an axe head or a hammer. In fact analysis of Iron Age tools does indeed show that such a technique was frequently employed.

'It would be much better to trade it in a solid lump,' John Rossetti pointed out, 'and you wouldn't get something like this perishing ingot coming out of a smelting furnace.'

The ingots are clearly emblematic swords, too thin and light as a rule actually to be fashioned into practical weapons, but perhaps attractive as trading tokens because of their resemblance to a prestigious finished article. In fact the habit of trading metal ingots in the likeness of working tools is widespread even today. In parts of West Africa, for instance, iron was, until very recently, still traded in the form of unfinished blanks for the manufacture of agricultural hoes, and hoe ingots have also been found on English Iron Age sites. But a kind of inflation sometimes sets in when the amount of metal employed in the ingot is reduced below the point where the object has any practical use. It becomes less than an ingot. It becomes money.

The two Johns were determined to put an end to their dependence on this second stage raw material and smelt the metal themselves from iron ore. They built a rather larger bowl furnace with curved retaining walls, rather on the lines of Martin's bronze furnace, but more completely covering the entire bowl. They stoked this furnace with charcoal and several pounds of iron ore, so arranging the ore that it would receive the heat created by the bellows draught but would not be oxidised by the inrush of air. Smelting must be done, they assured me, in a reducing, not an oxidising atmosphere. They then settled down to pump the bellows for six hours without stopping.

They seemed to achieve this feat without too much difficulty, each giving the other a break at intervals of three-quarters of an hour or so. But the sight of a squatting figure, covered in sooty grime for hour after hour, invited mental comparisons with the worst excesses of the Industrial Revolution. On a later occasion, when John Rockliff tried smelting a lump of iron pyrites found in a nearby field, the stench of rotting eggs was so strong that everyone else vacated the round house and he laboured in the stink and darkness alone.

This time the two blacksmiths worked together and produced, at the end of all their labours, a spongy mass of molten iron and shale which glowed stickily, like some white hot amoeba, in the bottom of the furnace. They fished it out with a small iron rake and tried to separate the stickier shale from the mass of iron. The next stage in the process called for the reheating and hammering of the 'sponge' of iron, to reduce it to solid metal. A day or two later they performed this task and after hours of hammering and beating they eventually produced a tiny fragment which as John Rossetti wryly confessed, was 'just about enough for a two inch nail.'

Some skills continued to defeat them. 'If I've learned one thing on this project,' Pete Little said to me one day, 'it is an enormous respect for Iron Age man. I hadn't realised when I started just how clever and ingenious and knowledgeable they were.'

Amen to that.

Chapter Fifteen

For nearly a week in February the whole of south-west England was enveloped in the deepest fall of snow for more than thirty years. Some roads were blocked by drifts more than twenty feet deep. The newspapers were full of accounts of isolated farms and villages completely snowbound and swiftly running out of essential supplies of food and fuel. Sheep and cattle were starving on the hillsides. Cars and trucks were blocked in and abandoned over thousands of miles of roads, and inadequate, rarely-used snowploughs inched slowly along the main highways, leaving the little side roads until last. The Iron Age village, isolated in the woods on top of the great sweep of snow-covered downland, was completely sealed off. Inquisitive newspapermen and television crews succeeded in snatching fleeting aerial views of the village in the rare breaks in the heavy cloud, but my own attempts to reach the project by helicopter were frustrated by bad weather.

After five days the film unit and I eventually got through by Landrover, only to find that we had been beaten to it by a heroic, embargo-breaking newspaper reporter. He had walked four miles through deep snow drifts, eventually locating the village by hearing the sound of an axe in the still air. The villagers had refused to let him in and he had been obliged to stand freezing half to death in the snow, conducting his interviews with the rather smug villagers outside the palisade, but from that moment on the isolation of the settlement was at an end. Visitors, some invited, some not, began to find their way through the woods to the clearing in the forest, first just a trickle of local people, gradually increasing in numbers until, by the end of March, dozens of rubbernecks were coming at weekends to stare at the settlement.

Mercifully, most of them were well-mannered and kept their distance. The life of the villagers was able to go on much as before, but their awareness of the outside world was obviously increased. Ironically, the five days of privacy in the snow when no one, not even the production team, had been able to visit them had been some of the most enjoyable of the entire project. This was especially true for those of them who had been looking for a challenge in the whole experience.

The goat byre and the remains of the grain stacks in February.

'It was great,' said John Rockliff. 'We had all the food we needed stored in the house. We were warm, because there was still plenty of wood about. We could look after the animals because they're all penned nearby. We felt completely self-sufficient. We didn't need anything from anybody.'

I told them of the villages, including the small town where I myself live, being cut off by snowdrifts.

'Well, that's the twentieth century for you isn't it,' said John. 'Nature puts a spanner in the works and the whole thing seizes up.'

Foot-long stalactites of ice hung from the thatch of the round house as the last of the snow cap melted from the roof. The ground was still frozen hard, and snow lay thickly under the trees. But the villagers were jubilant about the warmth and comfort of their home, even in the worst of weathers. Wrapped up in their sheepskins round the fire they could have survived almost Arctic conditions without taking any harm. In fact none of them had been ill since the previous summer. Only Jill, who now looked rather white and frail, had lost weight during the winter. The rest of them were plump and almost aggressively healthy.

'Well, we're pretty isolated from contact with infectious diseases here,' Martin explained, 'and our bowels move beautifully because of all that fibre, and there's a shortage of sugar, which is also a big improvement on modern diet. On the other hand we're obviously short on Vitamin C, or at least our Vitamin C levels are a lot lower than they would be in those people who are eating fresh fruit and vegetables all through the winter.' He laughed. 'Perhaps we'll all be going down with scurvy in a week or two.'

I asked them what kinds of food they missed.

'Fruit,' said Helen, longingly.

'Yeah,' breathed Sharon.

'Oranges, juicy things,' Helen's tone was dream-like.

'Tangy, tangy things I miss,' mused Martin.

'Yes,' agreed Sharon, 'spicy things we're very short of. But when we first started we had these amazing cravings for chocolate cake and things like that. Now we hardly ever seem to get them.'

All of them agreed that if they were to continue the project for another year they would reorganise the food supply completely, growing far more wheat, fewer peas and beans and laying in far bigger stocks of dried herbs, fungi and wild fruits. In the last few weeks their deer-depleted and rat-ravaged supply of wheat ran out completely. Their credit balance was almost exhausted and, after some argument, they agreed to manufacture a large surplus of saleable small pots in order to build up the credit to buy in more wheat, cheese and honey. I was anxious that the project should be viable on its own terms. It seemed to me that it did not matter particularly what surplus they could produce as long as they could demonstrate that they could do it. And as their level of skill improved it became obvious that they could continue indefinitely, paying their own way and providing for their own needs. They worked out that even if they paid modern currency for everything, their total needs, even including a few pints of beer, would not cost them more than about five pounds a week per head. When one considers the outcry today when wages in a Western country fall below forty pounds a week, it makes one realise just how affluent our society has become. On the project, living standards never fell to anything like Third World levels. No one was ever seriously in need of either food or shelter. But they did not fool themselves that all their material wants were satisfied, only their needs.

Sharon explained: 'I think life would be even happier here, if only . . . if only we had rubber boots, if only we had a few books, if only our parents and friends could come and see us. That's what I call the pursuit of happiness – if only . . .'

Martin felt that the twentieth century had produced some very

160

agreeable innovations. 'Not just medicine, but combine harvesters and nice big machines to take all that nasty work away and then you spend your time doing what you want.'

However hard the work may have been in the summer fields, the dark winter days gave them plenty of time to get on with the crafts and skills they really enjoyed. Brian had completed his lyre after countless hours of meticulous work, but the strings kept breaking. He had twisted threads of sheep gut and was trying different systems for stretching and drying them before fitting them to the instrument. They hung, like stout cobwebs, festooning the back door of the round house.

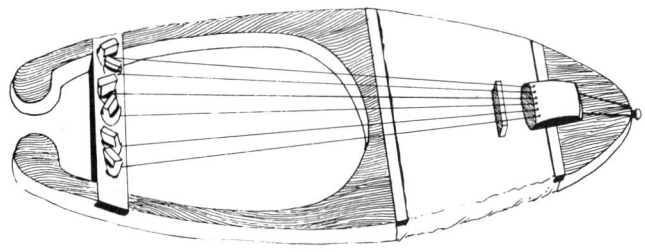

Brian working on his lyre.
Below, the finished instrument.

The girls had also made more progress with weaving and with sprang. Sharon, who did not rate her own skill with her hands very highly, had turned out a very creditable copy of a hairnet found in a peat bog at Forarden in Denmark. This net was found, still loosely attached to the coiled blond hair of the girl who had worn it in life over two thousand years before. It has been acclaimed by archaeologists as an example of the skilled craftsmanship of pre-historic people. 'It's quite interesting because most people who've studied it don't seem to be sure how it was worn,' said Sharon. 'But when we made it we found it was quite obvious.'

She bullied Sarah into putting the thing on for the sake of the film camera. 'I think it's a bonnet rather than a hairnet. It's the right size and there are drawstrings on three sides so it all gathers together very easily. The archaeologists said it was a luxury article, but it only took me three days, working with very fine wool. I don't see that it's a luxury item at all.'

Sarah had a loose-fitting jumper made of sprang which looked like an oversized tea-cosy and attracted rather unkind comments from the others. There were shawls and string bags as well.

'I er . . . made an overdress . . .' confessed Sharon hesitantly.

'And that's a string bag too,' cried Sarah. They both laughed.

Sharon had also tried her hand at basket making. Jill made very neat, strong baskets, which looked extremely hardy and professional when finished, and Kate could also turn out a useful article, but Sharon's basket was a wicker-work disaster area. Happy to clown around sometimes, Sharon insisted on displaying the hideous object for the camera.

'How on earth did you achieve that shape?' I asked.

'With difficulty,' she replied. 'My talents cannot be restrained. They branched out with free art form and broke away from the humdrum traditions of basket making! This,' and she held up the wretched thing for all to see, 'is a free form basket!'

Jill, on the other hand, worked with steady application. Almost everything she produced was well made, and the results of her tubular weaving, a triumphant pair of trousers for Pete Little, joined the rest of the wardrobe, which now included more woollen jumpers, woven skirts and cloaks than they actually needed. By March they could almost all dress, virtually entirely, in clothes made during the project. Linen continued to give them trouble, however. They had grown some flax, but not enough for their needs, and their efforts to ret it, beat it, and comb it out had not been a spectacular success. Brian Hawkins

The first stage of basket-making. Sarah is using withies for the base.

had obtained some hanks of treated flax and this they were able to spin into thread and weave into finished cloth.

'I'm really quite pleased with this piece,' said Jill, displaying the end result of her labours, a piece of cloth not much bigger than a pillowslip. 'It's quite a fine cloth, not a terribly even weave, but quite nice. I think it would be a bit scratchy next to the skin though,' she confessed, and went back to work again.

On the whole the crafts demanding robust labour fared better than those requiring truly delicate craftsmanship, though some of Brian's pottery was exquisitely decorated. By this time Brian and Martin had devised a refinement on the existing techniques. They produced two different kinds of ware, one heavy and coarse because of the large size of the inclusions in the clay and one much finer, grogged with fine sand ground almost to powder. On some of these finer pots Brian had incised delicate designs inspired by Iron Age originals, whorls, circles and cursive linear patterns. But it was the coarser wares that stood up to heavier use and higher temperatures.

'The only thing we still have trouble with is the really big storage pots they used to make,' said Brian. 'They seem to break up when we fire them, but I think it's only a matter of time, really.'

Jill and Sharon. The cone-shaped basket is a fish trap.

There was one technique in particular which they had still not mastered and did not look like mastering before the project finished. This was one of the most basic skills in the repertoire of almost all pre-historic peoples, the art of making fire. All of them at one time or another, but particularly John and Kate Rossetti, spent many hours trying to get a fire drill working. The drill they were using was only slightly modified from the one that they had tried and failed with at Beltain, nine months before. The hearth was a broad piece of softwood. The drill was made of harder wood, hawthorn or oak, delicately turned on the lathe. Kate and John would work away, Kate holding a little wooden cup over the top of the drill as a bearing and John sawing away for dear life with a bowstring wrapped around the drill. There was a mass of smoke but no fire until, in despair, I approached the expert with the most appropriate name in the business, the anthropologist, Dr James Woodburn. In the last weeks of the project Dr Woodburn demonstrated the correct technique and at last the villagers had the secret of making fire.

The trick was to use softwood, both for the vertical drill and for the horizontal hearth. After various attempts with other woods the villagers found willow best. The hearth, a piece of dry willow stick with one side chiselled flat, was held firmly on a flat surface by one of the villagers while another twirled the drill between the palms of his hands. The drill was about four feet long so that the hands could be rubbed slowly down its entire length. The technique demanded simply that the drill should rotate fiercely in a little hollow cut in the hearth. But the vital part was this: cut in the side of the hollow in the hearth was a small notch. As the drill was rotated a small trickle of hot sawdust fell from this notch and on to the flat surface below the hearth. For convenience this was usually a flat knife blade. After quite a short time, a minute or two at the most, the hot sawdust ignited. A quick handful of tinder – dried grass and wood shavings – cupped around the tiny burning pile of dust, a good deal of blowing and bingo, fire!

After countless hours of labour, failed experiment after failed experiment, and more intellectual effort than they had applied to most of their other problems, the solution had been demonstrated in one afternoon.

'Easy, isn't it?' said Martin.

On the days when the weather permitted it, Jill and Pete – on one or two occasions Jill and Sharon – would go out with the cows to plough. They had agreed, for the sake of the integrity of the project, that they should try and get the land ready for sowing, even though they would never be able to harvest another crop. The cows were now trained to such a pitch that they could be guided mostly by word of mouth, and though the big and cumbersome Betsy was still outpulled by the small and frail Jacky, they worked very much as a team. The technique of the human labourers had also improved enormously. The furrows now ran in straight lines across the fields and each square, of half an acre or so, was finely criss-crossed with intersecting scratches in the soil. Pete was quite pleased with the progress they were making. 'I think we are now finding that we could plough, rough plough, about half an acre a day. That's the sort of rate we are building up to, I think.'

Interestingly enough, half an acre is about the average size of the small square Celtic fields which can still be traced on the downs. The outline of the field edges is marked by lynchets, low banks which form as a result of the ploughing action. 'If we were to be a viable community we would have to cultivate about six or seven acres,' continued Pete, 'and I think we could do that with just the one team of cows, quite easily.'

They both agreed with the earlier diagnosis of food requirements, more wheat, fewer peas and beans, and thought that the heavier workload would be well within their capacity. 'We'd know what we were doing, second time around,' said Jill, sadly.

There was also some debate about the other farm activities, especially the livestock. Everyone agreed that if they were to have enough wool to clothe themselves they would need more sheep, though they believed they could build up their own flocks quite quickly. Cows were more of a problem. They needed them as draught animals and they needed bull calfs for rennet and to rear for beef, but the milk yield of the Dexters on their poor diet was dismally low. Betsy yielded about a cupful a day. Brigid and Jacky only gave about half a gallon in winter, but Brigid was rearing a calf so that in practice she produced even less. Only Mary, the old pure Dexter, produced over a gallon, and Mary was ill with a sadly terminal disease.

One dark afternoon, with several villagers standing by, they brought her out into the yard and fed her some hay. As she was munching contentedly away she was shot in the head and died without knowing what had hit her. Gloria the performing pig also met her end before the project was over and she, too, died without ever in her life having experienced a moment's disquiet. Both animals ended up in the cauldron or roasting in pieces over the fire and were eaten with equanimity. There was no cruelty at any moment on the project and not too much sentiment either.

The most successful animals from the husbandry point of view were probably the goats. On the whole, apart perhaps from Shaggy Maggy, they were very little trouble. They browsed contentedly in the woods most of the day and came in when they were called in the evening. Kate felt a warm regard for the goats. 'I think they've been more successful as milking animals than the cows really,' she said. 'They provide now at least as much milk and they eat much less hay, just grot around and eat anything that's coming up.'

New growth was in fact already starting in the woods as the worst of the winter weather tailed off and the days began to lengthen. The dog's mercury and the bluebells were already sprouting under the hazel, and clumps of snowdrops starred the ground, just as they had when the project began. When the hawthorn formed tiny sprigs of green on the end of its thorny twigs it was plain that spring was on the way. One morning there were two white kids in the goat house. Before the end of March there were eight, and out in the field the sheep too were beginning to produce the first, teetering lambs. It was almost time to go.

Chapter Sixteen

As the project entered its last few weeks there was increasing excitement. Visitors, long-missed friends and relatives were allowed in for the first time, and were duly dragged round in the mud to admire the animals and encouraged to sit in the choking smog of the round house, uneasily sipping herb tea out of the communal drinking bowl, or chewing hard on the nameless lump of meat from a spit roast. One wondered sometimes, looking at these clean loved ones in their shiny wellington boots, whether they were really enjoying their visit, once the exchanges of filial affection were over. But there were young people too with long hair and beards, perhaps a guitar, a sleeping bag to throw in the corner of the round house. They brought beer and admiration for the villagers and some of them were obviously envious of the relaxed and comparatively carefree life of the project.

But the visitors that aroused most speculation, possibly apprehension, were the archaeologists.

I had decided that many of those experts who had helped with advice in the beginning and some others whose views were more detached should be invited down to give their views of the project's accomplishments. One of the first to come was Peter Reynolds. His advice had been essential in the first place when the whole idea was conceived, but since that time he had come to feel that some of his own findings were being disregarded. He now objected, for instance, to the use to which we put the big round house and the fact that our little community with its twentieth-century outlook had no system of leadership struck him as particularly anachronistic.

'What we have here,' he said, 'is rule by committee, and I think in any kind of agricultural society this is so rare as to be almost non-existent. We must have a hierarchy and this we haven't got.'

Of course our intention from the first had been to try and explore the ways that modern people would adapt to Iron Age living conditions, not to try and recreate a Celtic household, but this remained the aspect of the project that was least generally understood.

Archaeology now combines many academic disciplines and different experts expressed interest in different activities. Professor Dimbleby, from the Institute of Archaeology in London, was intrigued by the way that the surrounding woodland had been exploited and how materials from it had been put to use in the village. He only regretted that the project could not go on for long enough to reveal more data. Richard Savage, from the Cheltenham College of Art and Technology, was interested in Martin's efforts at bronze casting, and Professor Ron Tylecote of Newcastle University took a similar interest in the iron work, because he had been the principal guide and mentor in this field at the beginning of the project. Dr Geoffrey Wainwright, who had himself excavated an Iron Age site near the village of Gussage All Saints, which had provided us with models for much of our experiment, was complimentary about the whole project.

'It's been a very rewarding experience,' he told me, 'normally archaeologists are just dealing with structural remains, post holes and pits and rubbish . . . and it's been interesting to be able to cloak these remains in some reality . . . just walking through the woods and coming upon the village . . . it gave one a very clear feeling of what it must have been like.'

The only thing that seemed to worry Dr Wainwright as he poked about the village was the absence of rubbish. 'Rubbish is my bread and butter,' he complained with a smile.

The villagers explained that they had very little to throw away.

'What about bones?' asked Dr Wainwright.

'We throw those to the pigs,' John Rockliff replied.

'But they can't eat them all . . .'

'Oh yes they can,' laughed the villagers.

In fact bones were used as knife handles, as needles and bodkins, though even these had a way of disappearing. The dogs probably knew a thing or two about that.

But the site was littered with small pieces of pottery, which somehow managed to get scattered over a very wide area as they were scuffed and brushed aside in the dirt, fragments of charcoal, flakes of daub from the buildings and carbonised grain – black and burnt where it had fallen into hot ashes. On more than one occasion a thorough sweep of the round house floor in search of a lost needle turned up many of these little charred grains. Interestingly they were always wheat or barley. Oats, being mainly used as animal fodder, never seemed to find its way into the fire. But the villagers were not on the site for long enough for the great accumulations of bone and pottery that are so much a feature of many Iron Age sites.

One item of rubbish that did accumulate in certain areas of the village particularly interested Professor Barry Cunliffe of Oxford University. This was burnt flint, flakes of the hard brittle stone, so common in chalk beds, which were burned almost black by contact with fire. Professor Cunliffe has a theory that these were used in connection with grain drying. As they sat with him in the round house the villagers explained their method of drying wheat in a sack on a shelf over the fire.

'We did try with flints,' said Sharon, 'only when the flints were very hot the grain just got burned, so we put hot flints and wheat in a bucket and sort of stirred it around and it worked OK.'

'Yes,' agreed Sarah, 'but it's an awful lot of work.'

'And the other unpleasant thing is that you get nasty sharp bits of flint in your flour,' added Jill.

'What about spreading skins over the hot flints and spreading the wheat over that?' asked the Professor.

The villagers laughed. 'The skins would get burned to blazes,' they all agreed.

Instead they demonstrated to Professor Cunliffe how flints got burned in the charcoal-making process, how, as the charcoal pit got larger with use, the flints, together with burnt earth, were thrown out of the pit and scattered over the working area. Over the course of years, they explained, very many of these would be likely to accumulate.

There was much more conversation of the same kind. The storage platforms on legs, for instance, a frequent subject for archaeological debate, were discussed as vermin deterrents. All agreed that smooth legs and overhanging platforms would help to keep rodents out of the grain store. They talked about threshing, about rubbish disposal, about pottery, the villagers all earnestly lecturing the Professor on his own field of study. Barry Cunliffe took it all in good part, putting more and more questions, listening with great attention to the answers. He may not have been entirely convinced by everything, but he did make the villagers feel that all their efforts had at least been of some interest to the professional archaeologist.

At the end of several hours of looking and listening I asked Professor Cunliffe whether he had found anything on the project that had been of value to him.

'They're all small things,' he told me, 'but together they add up to something quite considerable.'

He then explained how he had taken an interest in the little hollows in the earth, just inside the round house doors. These were made by chickens which came into the house, especially on wet days, and made use of the dry earth as a dust bath. 'Well, I can't now say that every scoop I find in an Iron Age house is a dust bath for chickens, but it makes me understand just that little bit more the conditions under which people lived, and the range of explanations that are possible.'

The archaeologists came and went, but the value of the project lay also in the kind of experience that the villagers themselves had gone through. Without exception they agreed that it had been enormously rewarding, though different people valued different things. Sarah and Kate had particularly enjoyed working with the animals. The two Johns and Pete Little seemed to feel that the chance to depend on their own skill to provide for themselves was the most valuable aspect of the project. Others, like Martin and Jill, felt that the experiment in group living was the most important thing. But whatever the serious value and whatever the privations the most noticeable thing about the village in its closing weeks was the fact that they were all thoroughly enjoying themselves. They worked harder than ever. Most people had a mental list of the jobs, little private experiments which they wanted to carry out before they had to go.

The last job they had to complete, a task that took the combined efforts of all the men and from time to time the women as well, was finishing off the cart. The great composite wheels were ready. The axle of apple wood was in position underneath the long Y frame, and the boards were dowelled into the top to make the cart bed. The wheels slid smoothly on to the greased axle, and were kept in place by great wooden washers and iron lynch pins. As a final refinement the walls for the cart bed were made out of woven hazel.

When it was finished at last, there was still one problem to be solved. 'We can't move it,' said Pete Little. 'The wheels alone must weigh a couple of hundredweight apiece. Let's hope the cows will manage it.'

In fact he was joking, but only just. The wheels looked very much in danger of bogging down in the deep mire around the palisade. The cows were brought out and with some difficulty yoked to the cart. To start with they strained uncertainly at the unexpected load, then slowly but sweetly the cart rolled forward. There was jubilation in the village.

The last few days were spent in a state of high excitement. There were visitors milling around the settlement, many of the animals had

Time to go – Kate wades through the mud.

already been returned to their owners or taken off to new homes and the place was no longer the same. Departure was in the air.

There was one small incident on the afternoon before the project was due to end that seemed somehow rather fitting. Emer, the large and lovable mongrel whose bass bark had kept many unwanted visitors at bay, was snuffling around the shrubbery on the edge of the clearing. Suddenly a rat leaped from a patch of bramble and raced over the open ground to another tangle of briars with Emer lumbering after it. She snuffled some more and the rat once more darted away, while Emer almost fell over herself trying to keep up. Then the rat panicked, turned and ran straight into her jaws. She snapped once, twice, and it was dead. It was Emer's first and only rat of the year, and it was as though she too had kept a list of things that had to be done before the project ended and now, at last, it was complete.

On the last morning of all the press, who had taken an increasingly strong interest in the television programmes, were at the gates soon after it got light. They had brought with them several bottles of champagne, which were duly popped while the cameras clicked. The villagers scooped up their belongings and trudged through the compound while the photographers ran ahead of them and begged them to walk this way or that, to stop, to smile. At the very last minute, as they staggered through the gate with their bundles, one of the polecats, Rush, disappeared from the basket which Jill had made for him and hunted off into the remains of a haystack in search of rats. 'Oh dear,' said Sarah. 'He doesn't want to go.'

'Do any of you?' I asked.

Some said no, some shook their heads and some just smiled sadly. But of course there was no question of the project continuing. The cover was blown, as it were; the landlord was anxious that the place should revert to tranquil woodland once again, and the villagers themselves wanted to return to the world. They trudged away up the track to the waiting vehicles. Behind them, for the first time in weeks, the village was bathed in the morning sunshine. Slanting low through the trees it shone brightly on the palisade and on the low roofs of the smaller huts, but the round house itself was in silhouette, surrounded by a glow of light where the great cone of the roof shut out the rising sun. From the top of the roof rose a thin plume of grey smoke, slowly curling upwards in the still morning air. No one had wanted to be the person who put the fire out.